Robert Noble

Two Trips To Heaven

One Man's Journey To The Other-Side

Two Trips To Heaven
One Man's Journey To The Other-Side
All Rights Reserved.
Copyright © 2013 Robert Noble
V5.0 r1.0

Noble Publishing

ISBN: 978-0-578-12518-3

PRINTED IN THE UNITED STATES OF AMERICA

Table of Contents

Dedication

This book is dedicated to my grandchildren, Antonio (Tony), Angelina (Lena) and Haven. I hope this book will give you some insight into who your grandfather truly was and this also is a reminder that anything can happen in life but it will take courage, determination and spirituality to persevere. I have done many things in my life and I have had many experiences. I have no complaints and I lived a life that some never had the opportunity to lead nor had the desire to take the risks for the returns that I have had and I wouldn't change a thing.

Here are some of the things I have done in my life and this is just a short list; I was a door gunner in the U.S. Navy on H-1 Huey's (helicopters). I have scuba dived to depths greater than 130 feet to see a ship wreck. I have been face to face with moray eels, sharks, barracudas, sea turtles, and octopi. I have seen a herd of wild horses charging through the Nevada desert. I have seen a flock of thousands of Blue Jays soaring through a forested canyon; I have seen mountain sheep ramming their horns in a territory dispute on top of a mesa. I have seen the wonder of the Mayan ruins in Mexico and the wonder of the great Sequoia National Forest in Northern California. I sat in awe on the shores of Lake Tahoe amazed by its beauty. I have seen majestic Eagles soar in the mountains of Alaska and stood on Glaciers at the Kenai Fjords and I stood at the edge of active volcanos in numerous places. There are so many things I still wish to see and experience. But, if it ends today, I had a good life.

Boating holds a prominent place in my life and I have raced in many Poker Runs, and offshore races. Boating has been a major part of my life both personally and professionally.

I enjoyed some of the pleasures that the world has to offer and visited places such as Cabo San Lucas, Puerto Vallarta, Cozumel, Playa Del Carmen, Cancun, Puerto Penasco Mexico. I have been to the Hawaiian Islands twice. I have been to the Bahamas', the Cayman Islands and Puerto Rico. I have been to the Alaskan Kenai Peninsula and the city of Anchorage, and it is an amazing place. I have been all over the Pacific Northwest and I have visited over 40 of the States in our great country. There are more places that I will see before I go.

I have held residences throughout the Chicagoland area, and in Bamberg South Carolina and Fairview Tennessee. I have also lived in Milton, Pensacola, Orlando, Jacksonville and Ft. Myers Florida and in Las Vegas Nevada, Scottsdale Arizona and Seattle Washington.

I have been fortunate to have had some great loves throughout my life. I have also been fortunate to remain friends with the majority. I have been blessed with love and hurt by it also. That, you should know, is how love goes. You will feel some pain throughout life, but pain is not a bad thing as long as it helps you grow and learn.

I have been blessed with a wonderful life but I have unfortunately seen some of the horrors that happen in life that most people should not or will not ever see. Those are not worth mentioning.

As you read these pages you will also see some of the challenges I have been through and survived. I have survived because of GODs grace and the determination by medical professionals but also through courage, determination and faith in my spirituality.

I have done many things and I can honestly say that at any given time, courage, determination and spirituality were always involved.

If you remember anything your Grandfather will ever say to you, remember these things:

Never let your dreams fall short and keep an open mind because there always is a way to make it happen. Don't be in a hurry because life gives you time and time is what you make of it. But also remember to never waste time because time is the one thing you cannot get back. Once it is gone, it is gone forever.

You will see it when you believe it, not the other way around. Have the vision to see your dreams and the courage to go after them. Don't be afraid to fail because failure is a teacher, learn from your mistakes.

Have the determination and courage to get up when you fall down and keep pursuing what you desire and love. Don't settle for second best you are worth the very best.

Maintain spirituality with GOD and understand there is more than the life we have on earth. Believe in his power and his glory and accept him into your heart and soul. He will help to guide you although at times you will question this, but never lose your belief, never lose your faith.

If you do these things you will have a wonderful life and enjoy what the world has to offer. So go out and make me proud, make your parents proud but most of all make yourself proud!

The last thing I wish to say to you, I can't take credit for, but it was told to me by a very intelligent and inspirational woman that you know, Bonnie Brake. It goes like this: "We have to keep an open mind, and an open heart, when our life on this world ends it is only for ourselves that we must answer, we will not be asked why anyone else has done things, only what WE have done.

Preface

How many chances are you supposed to get here on earth? The majority of people get one; they live their life, some live it with regrets some live it with great joy and then their time comes and life on earth ends and their spiritual life begins. I have been lucky enough to have passed over to the other-side twice and I am still here to talk about these tremendous experiences.

It was difficult to understand at first, yet I believe what had happened and I have accepted it in my life. It took two years to understand it and it took even more time to speak of it too people. Once I found a level of comfort with this experience, I was able to move forward in my life. I set aside what a glorious experience I had and held it tight in my memory.

Then six years, seven months and fourteen days later it happened again. The second time was more devastating and the process of understanding and accepting it started over again. This confirmed the knowledge that what had happened to me on August 15, 2005 was not a fluke. The same fears returned, the same trauma was there but this time it seemed to be larger and deeper.

Now that I am past the initial level of grief, I felt it necessary to tell my story so that others may believe in their experiences. When you speak to the skeptics, their face shows disbelief, yet curiosity soon surfaces. When I speak of my experiences, I find the reactions from people to be more inquisitive. I find that people want to know that there is something more after death. They are spellbound albeit skeptical by what I tell them. After all what had happened to me, happened twice so I have no doubts.

This will be a journey through the challenges of life, the agony and wonderment of death and the downside of free will that ends with shocking behavior. This will be a journey of spirituality, advice, history and knowledge. We will cross many paths throughout this story and on those paths we will explore our spiritual being and the challenges that it sometimes faces. Belief in your faith and belief in your GOD is all you need to accept what will occur to you after death. What is written in these pages is true. Nothing has been embellished for the sake of the story line. All the events within these pages did actually occur.

I want to thank my wife Lisa for standing at my side through some very difficult times. She has been my rock and my foundation. I will always cherish you and love you.

I wish to thank my friends and family for their enormous support throughout this long ordeal. A man does not need a lot of friends, he only needs friends of quality and I am blessed to have friends such as that.

I would also like to thank the men and women who worked so hard to save my life on two separate occasions. Special thanks goes out to my Cardiology team at NorthPoint Heart center in Berkley Michigan and to their Physician's Assistant, Ken Jackson, that worked diligently and never gave up to bring me back from death. You are my hero.

I wish to thank my therapist, Dr. Leitman, for helping me through times of fear, despair, and disbelief. She has supported me and helped me work through Post Traumatic Stress Disorder. She has helped me to see the forest through the trees.

I also wish to thank those that read this book and I hope my experiences can help you get through any similar challenges you are facing. I believe you will be able to take away something from this story that will help you in some way throughout your life.

Enjoy the Book!

1

Life in my Italian Family

An Italian wake and funeral is quite the event. There is the crying, the hugging, the color black and a lot of flower arrangements. In the 1960's and 1970's it was typically a 3 day event. The final day of the wake starts with a last visitation, the wailing at the coffin by the spouse and the priest will say prayers for the deceased. Then all the visitors are asked to get into their cars while the immediate family says their final goodbyes. They are then led to a limousine while the undertakers close the casket. The pall-bearers are asked to return to their positions around the casket and the casket is then carried to the hearse. Once the casket is placed in the hearse the funeral procession begins.

The procession departs the funeral home and drives by the deceased's home for one last look then the procession travels to the Catholic Church of choice. The pall bearers then carry the casket from the hearse to the vestibule of the church. The family and friends form the line behind the casket as it is wheeled down the aisle to the front of the church. The casket is then covered with a white blanket that typically has a cross embroidered on the blanket. The blanket symbolizes the white bib that we get when we are baptized, as our introduction to the church...the funeral symbolizes our entrance into heaven. The deceased person's feet are placed facing towards the altar and the priests are facing away from the altar as he stands and says mass. The reason for this is so their positions are reminiscent of their positions when they were alive and celebrating Mass together. The Priest will say some prayers and then circle the casket with holy water and then incense. The incense is very scriptural, very Roman Catholic, and very Judeo-Christian.

The reason for the use of incense is the smoke of the incense carries our prayers up to heaven and to the Lord. The funeral mass then begins as a traditional Catholic mass which will last approximately an hour.

If you are an Italian in the Chicago area your burial is more than likely at Queen of Heaven or Mt. Carmel cemeteries in suburban Hillside, Illinois. If the deceased is to be placed in a mausoleum crypt, then the procession stops at the cemetery chapel. The casket is taken into the chapel, those that are there for their last respects will gather around the casket. The priest is there and more prayers are said. Once that is complete, you then have the option to see your loved one interred or you could let the cemetery staff complete the burial on their time schedule. For an in-ground burial the procession goes to the graveside when the casket is placed on a rack with a lowering device and after the prayers are said the casket is lowered into the grave. Once the burial is complete then the group will usually go to a restaurant for a catered luncheon.

From a young age we were used to seeing deceased people in their coffins. Death was never kept from us as children. It was meant to show us respect for those that have passed on and respect for the family that suffered the loss. We always believed the deceased was in a better place but we never knew if that place actually existed or how it was better than where we were. It was always taken in faith, the Catholic faith. Seeing the bodies lying in their coffins, realizing that they would never be back again was always upsetting but somehow in a child's eye, life just continued on. As we get older and grow into adults, death always seemed harder to accept. I suppose it is the acceptance of our own mortality or the fear in our mind that asks the question-am I next? As we begin to lose our own friends the questions start all over again. We still wonder if they are in a better place. We hope they are but does anyone really know for sure?

My biological grandfather was Francesco Federici, who died at a young age. We don't know much about him but what we do know was that Grandpa Frank was married previously and had 4 children. His wife, Filomina, had died and as the story goes, Grandpa Frank knew my Grandmothers brother and they sent for Lucia from Italy. She arrived on the ship the Ancona on August 30, 1915 at the age of 22. We also know they were officially married 2 days after her arrival in the U.S.A. Grandpa Frank died March 25, 1926 from bronchial pneumonia. He left Lucia with 6 small children to care for. My Grandmother 'remarried' Pete Guagliano and one more child was then born.

Pietro Gualiano was the only Grandfather we knew. He was a tall thin man, he spoke very little English and what he did try to speak was very broken. But somehow, you always knew what he was saying to you. What we do know about his immigration to Chicago does have some mystery surrounding it.

On his immigration to the USA in 1922, at the age of 27, he lists a wife, Laura, in Italy on the ships manifest and the mystery begins. On his WWII draft card it lists Mrs. Laretta Guagliano as a primary contact but at my Grandmothers address. Are Laretta and Laura the same person? It would be logical to assume they are the same person since Italians were known to change names to a more American version. We haven't found any records of a Laretta Guagliano coming to the United States or on any census records? Did they live with Grandpa Frank and his first wife Filomina? Did Laretta die here and was she returned to Italy with Grandpa Pete to be buried in the homeland? Did Pete take over for Grandpa Frank and then he became our Grandfather? As in all genealogy there are a lot of questions.

We do know he made two trips to the U.S.A. His second and final return was in 1930 aboard the Conte Biancamano. There was no further mention of a wife in Italy on that ships' manifest.

We do not know if Grandma and Grandpa Pete's marriage is official, as there are no records stipulating their marriage in Cook County Illinois. They lived as man and wife until Grandpa Pete died in April, 1968.

The fact remains that Grandma Lucia took the last name of Guagliano for the rest of her life, and social security and death records from the state of Illinois list her as Lucia Guagliano. It is another mystery of our family. But, Grandpa Pete loved all of us kids and one would be no wiser from viewing our family that he wasn't our real Grandfather.

We all lived on Chicago Ave in two story apartment buildings. At 2527 W. Chicago Ave. on the first floor was my Aunt Theresa and Uncle Sam and Grandma Lucia and Grandpa Pete lived on the second floor. Next to them my Aunt Sue and Uncle Angelo lived on the second floor.

My family lived next to them on the first floor. At this time my other Aunts' and Uncles lived away from Chicago Ave. Uncle Tony lived on the South Side of Chicago, Uncle Pat on the Northwest side of Chicago, Aunt Arcy was in Hillside, Illinois a western suburb of Chicago and Aunt Millie was in Phoenix, Arizona.

In the back yard of this little property on Chicago Ave, Grandpa Pete grew a garden that was to be revered in the neighborhood. He was the master at gardening. He had two huge fig trees, countless tomato plants, cucumbers, lettuce, various pepper plants not to mention the fresh basil, oregano, thyme, parsley and other herbs. The plants were always full and producing their harvest. He was also a very well-known wine maker. The basement was divided into 5 separate sheds and a common area. The last 3 sheds were off limits. They were filled with 50 gallon wooden barrels of fermenting 'Dago Red Wine".

It wasn't too much longer that my Aunt Theresa and Uncle Sam bought their own home in the western suburbs and my parents and I then moved below Grandma and Grandpa.

I have very vivid and happy memories of Grandpa Pete. I was very close to him and living below them and being by them every day made the bond stronger. When I was about 5 or 6 years old we went into the garden and picked figs and tomatoes. We took them down into the basement. He had a little table down there and he cut up the figs and cut the tomato into slices with his handy pocket knife that I still have to this day. He poured himself a small glass of wine and poured me a little wine in a shot glass. We sat there and ate figs and tomatoes and sipped wine. I remember my Mother coming downstairs to do laundry and saw us sitting there. She complained to Grandpa that he was giving me wine, all said in Italian of course. Words were yelled back and forth, I didn't understand a word of it but she left, we stayed and finished our figs, tomatoes and wine.

My Aunt Reta and her husband Al Wagner were a very important part of my life. They raised my father from when he was about 8 years old after his mother died and his father left. They had a summer home in Northern Illinois on Fox Lake that we would spend our summers at. It was a great place to be a kid, but the only problem was, I was the only kid. I always had to keep myself occupied and entertained. It was actually kind of lonely.

Grandpa Pete often came along to help around the property. We had 3.5 acres of lawn to cut, countless trees to prune and we needed the help. Grandpa Pete loved to fish and he would catch channel catfish and we would have fresh fish for dinner. I would always sit with him at the seawall with my little bamboo pole in the water.

He would talk to me in Italian, tell me stories that I didn't understand but it was OK. The words didn't mean anything it was the time we spent together. I had a French bulldog named Lucky. He would come and hang out with Grandpa and me. But Lucky had other motives. Grandpa would pull in a nice catfish and put it into a bucket full of water. Lucky would sneak up and snatch a catfish and run like hell. Apparently Lucky liked fresh catfish also.

Grandpa Pete would run after that dog cursing in Italian but was never able to catch him. So Lucky would have his catfish meal and we would go back and catch some more fish sitting on the seawall talking without understanding a word.

There are so many other memories' but here is the last one for now. He liked to go down to Lake Michigan and catch smelt, a small sardine like fish. He would use a net to catch them. We would wake early and he would take me on the bus down to the Oak Street beach area. There, we would net buckets full of smelt. When we had our buckets full, we would get back on the bus for home. The smell of the buckets of fish was horrible and the other passengers always complained. Grandpa didn't care, he would just laugh.

These are memories you simply can't replace. Grandpa Pete died when I was 10. It was difficult to say goodbye and to know that there would be no more memories being made with him. His funeral though was one that would rival a true Mafia funeral. It took two flower cars to carry the wreaths and flowers and his funeral procession was almost a mile long. It was a true testament to the character of this man. He didn't have any money but was wealthy in friends and family.

Before Grandpa passed on and after, you could always smell the fresh made bread coming from Grandma's kitchen. Grandma didn't speak English very well either but you always knew what she meant. She was loved, and she loved us unconditionally. She was short and heavyset. She always wore her hair up and wore glasses. She was caring and compassionate and the funny thing is, she was a lady with a fun personality but in pictures she would never smile. Grandma Lucia was the foundation of our family, and our matriarch. When she got ill, my Mother had to care for her and we moved Grandma into my bedroom and I moved upstairs into her apartment. When Grandma Lucia passed away our family changed and will never be the same.

Grandma and Grandpa's apartment was the central gathering point for all holidays. I can still see the apartment. It was long and thin, on one side was three bedrooms and the other side was the kitchen, one bathroom, the dining room and living room. Grandma, Grandpa would have six of the seven children and their spouses, and all the grandchildren in this little apartment on holidays.

There were over 30 people in this apartment on Chicago Ave. and amazingly, it was always comfortable. The best memories were of Christmas Eve. The snow would be falling over Chicago Ave. and the famous Chicago wind was blowing hard. The Christmas tree was in the corner by the front windows next to the fireplace all covered in silver tinsel and ornaments and large colored Christmas lights. All the cousins of my generation and younger would be looking out the front windows hoping for a glimpse of Santa Claus and his Reindeer through the falling snow. As you look back from the front window into the apartment there was always a flurry of activity. You could smell the food, it was simply amazing.

The adults would be at the 'big' table and the kids were at little tables throughout the house. We would start with a variety of cheeses such as Romano, Provolone, Mozzarella, Asiago, Fontina, and regular American cheeses', also pepperoni, salami, dry sausage and prosciutto and fish appetizers, and then move onto Pasta Fazool or polenta and followed by a huge salad. The first course would be a pasta dish like lasagna or ravioli. Of course you had fresh Italian sausage and home-made meatballs. Then the main course would be a ham or turkey or possibly a big roast beef my Father would cut special for the occasion (he was a butcher). After this feast and flurry of food, the women would be clearing the table from the nights feast. Then they would bring out the coffee, milk, homemade Italian cookies, cakes, and can-noli's. Fresh fruit was abundant and the roasted walnuts and hazelnuts were everywhere.

The kids would be running in and out of the dining room and kitchen grabbing cookies and getting their piece of cake. The house was loud and if seen by an outsider they would think it was highly unorganized but it was the exact opposite.

I can see the table to this day. At the head of the table was Grandpa Pete sipping his glass of Dago Red, Uncle Angelo smoking his cigarette, sipping a coffee and cracking hazelnuts, Uncle Pat sipping his martini and smoking a cigarette, Uncle Eugene peeling an orange and sipping a scotch, Uncle Sam smoking a cigarette and drinking his scotch, Uncle Tony drinking some wine with Grandpa and splitting a tangerine. My Father would be smoking a cigar and drinking a Brandy Alexander and then of course my Aunt Reta was with all the men and she had her own Brandy Alexander. Aunt Reta rarely did domestic chores. Of course all the Aunts smoked too. With all the smoking in the house, it was amazing you could see at all or smell the incredible food, but you could! You could smell the cookies as if some of them just came out of the oven. It was a time that was the true description of a family Christmas and when Grandma and Grandpa passed on it was changed forever.

One last item of life on Chicago Avenues experiences was the death of my Father. It was 1977; he was always a sickly man, and he passed on at 58 years old. He was the first of the siblings or their spouses to pass away. He died of a heart attack. It was his second. He went into the bathroom and never came out. My Mother on the other hand smoked for 60 years, she has had one heart attack and two strokes. She just turned 93 in October of 2012 and is as well as can be expected for her age. (see chapter 17)

We argued a few days prior to his death. It was a severe argument and we didn't talk for days. The night before he passed, he did say to me that no matter what he still loved me, I didn't respond.

This has been a hard piece of guilt to carry all these years. The following morning I woke early and went down to swear into the US Navy. As I was waiting for my groups turn to swear in, three of my Uncles came in and said that we were leaving. I refused and stood my ground with my Italian hard headedness.

Then they said my Father had died and I needed to come home. It was a devastating time filled with confusion, sadness and shock. When my Father died it left a large hole in my heart. I think a little piece of me died with my Father that day. It wasn't easy as a young boy, my Father was sickly and couldn't do some of the things other Dads could and my parents were older. I was born when they were nearing 40 years of age. I think at some point we all doubt our parents' love for us. But I knew he loved me and I knew he would be terribly missed. I was 19 when he died and that is a difficult time for a young man. A father's guidance was necessary to navigate this time between boyhood and adulthood. I didn't have that luxury. I am 55 years old today and I miss him as much today as I did in 1977.

The neighborhood we grew up in was called 'The Patch'. It was primarily an Italian neighborhood in the inner city of Chicago. We knew we lived in the big city but it felt smaller, it felt more like a small town atmosphere. Everyone knew which kid belonged to whom. You couldn't be too naughty because the telephone call would be home before you got there. It was a wonderful neighborhood to grow up in and that level of family and closeness that we all had will never be replaced. When we started kindergarten at Holy Rosary Catholic School, your classmates were with you until you went off to High School. To this day I still keep in touch with at least 10 of my former classmates. It was a better time back then and I can only hope that my Grandchildren can experience something similar at some point in their lives.

2

Understanding Religions

What happened to me, not once, but twice are true stories. There is more than our meager life here on Earth than we know of. I have always been inquisitive and had a thirst for knowledge. I have learned to be very good at investigation and research. I have always believed there is an answer for everything and we just had to find it. I always believed at getting right to the point of things and going at a project straight on. I can move through diversity quickly and I somehow seem to come out of it for the better.

These struggles that I have endured are steeped in spirituality and my belief in a being greater than myself. I am struggling to make it back once again but as I get older the path back this time is harder. I am confident I will find the right path and this book is part of this journey.

I was born and raised in Chicago Illinois into an Italian family and into the Roman Catholic religion. I attended church regularly, I attended a Catholic grammar school, I was an altar boy in my church and then I attended an all-boys military high school where church attendance was mandatory. I was instilled with the Catholic version of Heaven and Hell and Purgatory where we will atone for our sins before being granted access into the grace of GOD. If we were bad we would face the deamination of Hell and suffer for all of eternity. As all young

Catholic children we believed in the Ten Commandments and the horror we would face if we in fact broke them. We knew no other religion. We knew no other way to be. We believed what we were taught as Catholic children.

We were trained to be Catholic and all other religions were just a mystery and were not spoken of. The good part about being Catholic, and an Italian Catholic at that, was the ability to go to confession and Monsignor Pelicore would wipe the slate clean so we can start all over again. Getting a do-over was a great feeling. But this was for the minor sins only. A few Hail Mary's and a couple of Our Father prayers and we were atoned for our sins.

When I attended Carlisle Military School in Bamberg, South Carolina I was one of four "northerners" and one of only eight Catholics in the school. Being out of my element was culture shock enough but I was also in the Deep South where a whole other culture was in place and as a young boy from Chicago going to a small town in the Deep South, well, shock was an understatement. Looking at an entire student body and there were only eight Catholics? Well, I thought to myself, what else was there? I soon found that there were many different religions.

As a 'minority' Catholic we attended our service on Saturday evenings. We didn't go to a church since there wasn't a catholic church in the town at that time. Our service was held on Campus in a classroom where a priest came to us to keep us in the Catholic grace of GOD.

The remainder of the student body would rise Sunday morning go to the chow hall for breakfast then get into formation according to their religious affiliations and march off to their various church services for the day. They would return to campus later that evening. The rest of us ('Catholics') would remain on base on Sunday's. Lunch was always a table for eight. The day was always boring. We always waited for the rest of the students to arrive back on campus so we can hear the stories of their day. Regardless of their religious beliefs they were always off campus in the presence of the town folks, and around the town girls! They were often taken in by families from their churches and fed a good meal or taken to picnics after church. The 'eight' could only live vicariously through their stories.

Being a 'northerner' and of course not quite submissive, I came to the conclusion that it wasn't quite fair that the other students were having such a great time and I had to stay on campus on Sunday's.

The next Sunday morning I woke up, had breakfast and then got into the Methodist formation with my friends and marched off to their church services. I would then alternate my Sundays. One would be for Baptist, one for Methodist, one for Protestant, one for Lutheran, one for Pentecostal and one for Black Baptist. It was an education unto itself. The Baptist and the Methodists were the major religions in that little town. I would attend one of those two churches on a more regular basis than the others. We were fed well, we got to intermingle with the local girls and the local boys were none too happy about that. I did attend the Pentecostal church once or twice but I found it a bit over the top for me.

The Methodist, Protestant and the Lutheran churches I found to be quite similar to my faith and in the same style of the service but the Baptist's were a bit more energetic. The services were more involved and entertaining. You were drawn into the minister as he preached. You had to listen and interact with the service and when you left church you felt that the hand of GOD reached down and touched you. But I learned from them all, and we all had but one GOD, the same GOD.

I did not mention the Black Baptist Church in the last paragraph because it is a story unto itself. Since there were only four Northerners in the school two of the other three were African American. Both were the first black students in the schools 100 year history. I did say the school was in the Deep South. One of the two boys was from Ohio and we were in the same grade. The other was a younger student. DeWayne and I became fast friends. We played on the baseball team, basketball team, track team and we were co-captains of the football team together.

Being in the Deep South the Black students were not allowed to attend the regular Baptist Church service but had to attend the Black

Baptist church on the other side of the tracks. Yes, there was a division by railroad tracks.

I did say it was culture shock earlier and I was not joking. One Sunday I decided to join DeWayne for church services. I placed myself in formation with the Black Baptist students; I must say I did get quite a few looks from the rest of the student body. I didn't think twice about it and off we went to the Black Baptist Church in Bamberg, SC.

I was welcomed into the church although I stood out like a fly in a bowl of grits. Of course I got the standard double take from the congregation but that soon passed. The music started and they sang, hollered, and danced and prayed. The preacher was more powerful and forceful than the white Baptist church minister. I was mesmerized by his character and his mannerisms. It was truly riveting. Then after the service the local women would take us home for a good old fashioned southern BBQ. The food was this side of Heavenly. I learned to eat a variety of different things I never heard of, collard greens, turnip greens, fried Okra and even chitterlings (although not my favorite). We also ate the standards such as beef and pork ribs but they also prepared things like squirrel, possum and rattlesnake. It was quite the culinary excursion. I do not believe I ever felt as welcomed as I did in their Church and homes as I felt those times in 1975.

This was an eye opening experience for me. I could not understand why they did not see or frankly care about the color of my skin as the people in the other Baptist Church cared about the color of theirs. I started to understand the world a little more and it was a different world in South Carolina. Up north the Blacks lived in our neighborhoods and attended our Catholic church and some attended our Catholic school. We were used to seeing them and talking to them. But in South Carolina it was different.

They were separated. DeWayne and I couldn't go into the same restaurant in town and sit together; we were always looked at differently when we were in town together. It was a different world and a different time then.

I was dating a girl from the next town over in Denmark, SC. One

Saturday night we went out and I brought DeWayne. We introduced him to one of her girlfriends. We would double date together. The only problem was this girl was white and of course DeWayne was black. We couldn't go into town to the little movie theater or out for dinner. We had to stay on campus and go to the Non-Commissioned Officer's (NCO) club where we could watch T.V. or listen to music and be together. It wasn't easy to keep their relationship from the other students on campus and some did not think very highly of that relationship but we dealt with it.

At half time of our Junior Homecoming football game it was tradition to announce the players and their dates. After I was announced the announcer introduced DeWayne and his date and when he walked onto the field with her, there was silence in the stadium. It was unnerving and the staff at Carlisle Military School was not amused. Colonel Waddy Thompson was the second in command at the school and he was also my direct supervisor since I worked on the Battalion Staff which he ran. Colonel Thompson was ironically the only staff member who was Catholic. He wasn't very pleased with DeWayne and my actions that evening. After the game DeWayne and I received a severe talking too on the difference between white and black in the South. After DeWayne was dismissed Col. Thompson asked me how long I was attending the different church services. When I told him since the beginning of the school year, let's just say, he wasn't too pleased with me. From that night forward, I was given a new assignment under the guise of my Battalion Staff job.

My new job was to take roll call each and every Sunday morning and insure that all students whom were not on sick call were in formation to attend church and all students were to check in with me upon their return from church to insure all cadets were accounted for. This job restricted me to base and my Sunday church adventures had officially ended. I did not think what Col. Thompson did was wrong. I saw it as nothing more than an order I had to follow as we were trained in the ways of the military. None the less, it hurt because I no longer had the freedom, the food and the interaction with the locals.

Colonel Thompson was one of the greatest men and mentors I have ever known. He was also an excellent teacher and a friend. He was firm when needed but held more compassion than most. I held a great respect for this man and I am thankful that I had the honor to know him and learn from him. I remember his portly body on a quick pace about campus with his pipe in his mouth, a stern look on his face and his military style return salute. It was as if he was always on some sort of mission as he scurried about campus.

His southern drawl was soothing yet forceful when need be and when he taught class he was considerate and patient. He cared about the boys that were placed in his care. He watched over all of us and kept us in line. If we crossed that line we were insured a solid paddling from the Colonel. Life was different then and it worked. Afterwards he would talk to you and try to help you understand why that had to happen and how not to let it happen again but in a fatherly tone. I once, only once had that displeasure. I learned from that experience as I would have learned from my own father back in Chicago.

I still think of the life lessons he taught us and the care he had for us. He always made us feel like we were one of his own children. He did write a book about his time at Carlisle and I still have that book to this day. It is my way of remaining close to a mentor, a friend and a leader.

In 1976 I started to separate from the Catholic religion and expand my mind that not all I had learned as a Catholic was correct and that other options were acceptable. I have never abandoned my Christianity or my belief in GOD. I just parked my Catholicism and journeyed out on my own exploration of faith.

I had some doubts about religion in general and what to really believe about GOD. I was on a quest to learn more and it took many more years of exploration and those lessons were brought to the forefront one evening in 2001 when my Godfather was on his death bed in Illinois.

3
The Voice of GOD

I was living in Gilbert Arizona in 2001 when I received a phone call from my cousin Tim that his Dad, my Godfather, had taken a turn for the worse. I immediately booked a flight to Chicago for the next day. In the Italian heritage a Godfather is well respected as he takes the place of ones Father in the event of the Fathers death. Uncle Sam was my second Father.

I believe I arrived into Chicago's Midway airport about 7:00 PM. My cousin Tim picked me up and took me straight to the hospital. My Aunt Theresa (Uncle Sam's wife) was there; my Mother was there as well as my Uncles other son Sam, his wife and their children. I went into the room to see Uncle Sam. He looked frail and struggled to breathe. It was as if you could feel death circling and just waiting for its turn. I went back into the waiting room, and I said my hello's to all that was there. In true Italian fashion the waiting room was like an Italian restaurant. It was filled with food; Italian Beef, Italian Sausage, rigatoni, mostacholi, salad and bread. No matter how bad things are, Italian's always have food available. It eases our pain. We also want to take care of the staff, not because we feel they will care for our loved one any better, but out of respect since Italians have a habit of taking over an area. We also respect the job the hospital staff does and we know it is difficult.

As the night wore on we could see my Aunt and my Mother were getting tired and my cousin's children were getting anxious. About 11 PM they all went home to get some rest and Tim and I decided to spend the night with his Dad.

We were going to sleep in the waiting room just in case something happened through the night. Tim and I talked for a while more, we ate a little more, we checked on Uncle Sam two or three more times. It was quiet on the floor. The midnight shift was on duty, there were two nurses at the nursing station. The halls were deaf with activity.

We decided to try and get some sleep on the most uncomfortable vinyl sofa's that were ever produced. I was having difficulty sleeping. I looked over at Tim and he was asleep. It was going on 2 A.M. I was drifting in and out.

Suddenly I heard this powerful yet soothing voice. It was controlling yet loving, it was authoritative yet compassionate. The words were loud and clear. The voice said; "Sam, come home." I will never forget the sound of that voice and the way that voice made me feel. It startled me but I wasn't afraid. It was strange to me but known at the same time. It was forceful but I felt the love in its tone. Never have I heard nor felt the command that voice proclaimed.

It wasn't like the movies when the voice echo's, It was just a voice, albeit powerful. I sat straight up and immediately looked about. I thought this was a horrible joke someone was playing. I stood and looked down the hallways. All the hallways were empty, there was no activity. I looked at Tim and he was a sleep. I looked for the nurses and both of them were still in their seats at the nurses' station apparently on the computers.

I thought to myself that I was dreaming but the voice was too powerful and strong. I sat there staring blankly at the wall. Had I just heard the voice of GOD? It was now about 4 A.M. I didn't know if I should wake Tim or not. I decided to let him sleep. I was afraid to go back to sleep, I didn't know what would happen next. I knew at that moment that I did in fact hear what I thought and I knew he was preparing Uncle Sam for his trip home. It was truly the voice of GOD.

Uncle Sam was always a strong man and he fought for his life. It was just before 6 P.M. that he lost his battle and passed on. When the family and friends left Tim and I walked his Father, my Godfather to the morgue. We cried all the way there. But we knew we had to complete this task out of love and out of respect for a great man. It was the right thing to do.

My Aunt Theresa is a devote Catholic as many in my family are. I know she was taking his loss hard and that was to be expected. Our hearts were also heavy with his loss. He was a good man. He was a man of few words but many looks. He had a way of just looking at you with a whiff of anger and a smudge of disappointment and you knew to correct your actions immediately. He had a good sense of humor and I can see his warm welcoming smile to this day.

It was a few days after his funeral was over when I sat down and had a talk with my Aunt Theresa. I told her what I had heard that fateful night she lost her husband. She looked at me with a strange expression and I thought she would say I was imagining it or I was oobatz (crazy).

She took a few moments as if to absorb what I just told her and she looked me right in the eye and said "Robert, you heard the Voice of GOD."

My life changed that night. It had nothing to do with various religions. It had nothing to do with being raised and taught in the Catholic ways. It was a moment in time that few have had the honor to experience. I have always questioned the stories of the miracles mentioned in the bible. I believe that is because those same miracles do not happen in today's world. I can't say exactly why I was chosen that night to hear his voice. I can only speculate that I needed to hear his voice to give me the faith I was seeking and for me to acknowledge his true existence for what was planned for me in the future.

To this very day that voice is profoundly in my memory. I can still hear and feel its power and compassion. I have not heard it again throughout all the challenges I have went through in the past 7 years.

I know if I do hear that voice again, it can mean my real final moments on earth are near. I believe that it could be GODs way to call us home and no matter how talented the people are that try and save our earthly bodies, they will ultimately fail.

When GOD calls we will happily go, deservingly to the other side. We will go 'home' and our soul will be closer to GOD from our learning's here on earth.

4

The First Event

I was still living in Arizona; my daughter was living in Fort Myers Florida. My grandson, Antonio, was 1 ½ years old at that time and my daughter just had my granddaughter Angelina. I was trying to get a job with a boat dealership group there so I could be closer to the kids. I got hired by a dealer group and made my way to Florida. I was supposed to be en-route to Clearwater, Florida to manage the dealership there which is about an hour north of Fort Myers. But on my trip across country I was detoured to the Jacksonville dealership to take that over for a short time. I was there for a few months and unfortunately my daughter got into a bit of trouble and the kids were taken into custody by the Florida Department of Child and Protective Services (DCFS).

While I was in Jacksonville I traveled to Fort Myers to see my grandkids and speak with the case worker for DCFS. It appeared she was willing to work with me to gain custody of Antonio and Angelina and get them out of foster care. After a couple of months of negotiating, at the last moment, DCFS changed their mind and would not release them to me in Jacksonville. They felt it was too far out of their supervisory area. Since FDCFS is a state wide agency, this made absolutely no sense. But, none the less I was denied. I spoke with my supervisor and explained my situation. He then spoke with the president of the company and they decided to make a change in management and give me the Ft. Myers dealership.

I arrived in Ft Myers on a Monday morning about 7 AM and checked into a motel for the time being. I just drove five hours and now had to break down a boat show they had that weekend. I met the new staff, and that evening went shopping for an apartment. On Tuesday I signed the lease for a new apartment and on Wednesday evening I had the DCFS case worker inspect the furnishing to insure it was satisfactory to their standards.

Thursday evening the case worker delivered the children to me. I was a Dad again. I saw Antonio when he was born and one time after that on a visit to Chicago. I saw Angelina just once right after she was born. I was forty six years old, I have been divorced for quite some time, I haven't raised children or changed a diaper in over twenty years, I am in a new city and in four days, I took over a dealership as the General Manager, I got an apartment, furnished it and now have custody of a two year old and six month old. I think my level of stress greatly expanded in no time at all.

The children were at a daycare in a local church. DCFS was paying for that on behalf of the foster parents. Once I retained custody and through some negotiations, the Department of Children and Family Services agreed to pay for day care at the Christian Day Care facility on my behalf. This was a great relief.

When I first arrived in Ft. Myers, I went to the daycare to see the kids while I was arranging for the apartment and furnishings. I saw Antonio first and he remembered me but was too busy playing to care. The next stop was the infant room to see Angelina. One of the young girls on staff there was holding Angelina. I suppose my next question through them for a loop and showed them just how much I did not know about the situation I was about to undertake. I asked them, what does Angelina eat? Now that wasn't a bad question, there are a variety of baby foods on the market. Their response was she eats stage one or stage two. I guess the expression on my face said it all.

They said, "You have no idea of what you are doing, do you?" Well the answer to that was a simple 'no'. They asked if I had a credit card and on their lunch break they took me to Walmart and took me shopping to buy the proper foods, diapers for both kids, and other items I would need. It all worked out and they also baby sat for the kids on the weekends when I had to work.

Our routine was military like. I woke early and got myself prepared for work. I woke the kids, washed them, fed them their breakfast and took them to daycare by 7:30 AM. I then either went to the grocery store to stock up on items or went to work by 8:00 AM.

Our dealership closed at 6:00 PM, but I had to leave by 5:45 PM to pick up the kids by 6:00 PM when the daycare closed. When we got home; I would play with them for a bit, and then give them their baths and then prepare their dinner. I would let them play a little more while I prepared their lunches for the next day and their backpacks with extra clothes and diapers. Then it was quiet time and bed time.

After I got them to sleep, then it was my time for dinner, then laundry and off to bed and it started all over again. On Saturday I would drop them at the sitter or the sitter would come to my house until I got off work. Sundays, was just a normal day, take them to the park, car rides, the beach etc.

I had some close older friends in Michigan that I had met when I lived in Las Vegas many years earlier. I also dated their daughter in Las Vegas. Well, they were like a Mom and Dad to me so I called them as I always did and told them about my new found family. Steve then put his daughter on the phone. We hadn't talked for years. She recently had a little boy who was about 1 years old at that time. She helped me understand how to feed the kids a healthier diet, how to make certain foods, and how to deal with certain situations.

One day in January of 2005, I did the normal routine, dropped the kids at daycare, went to the grocery store dropped the groceries off at home and then headed into work. My office manager and my salesman said to me, "you don't look so good." I felt OK, just a little run down, but my chest had heaviness to it. They suggested I go get checked out so I drove to a small hospital with chest pains and I was rushed in to

ER. After the hooked me up to the numerous machines and inserted the multiple I.V.s, I immediately called the DCFS case worker and told her what was going on and she came right over to the hospital. After some initial tests it appeared I had a minor heart attack. She told me she would have to put the kids back into foster care until I was able to be released and care for them once again. Well that wasn't the right answer. I tried to discharge myself but the hospital would not allow it.

I then called the daycare center and got the case worker to agree to leave them in my custody if one of the girls from daycare agreed to take care of them until we get through this medical situation. That was an applicable solution to all and we were able to side-step this issue.

The hospital I was at did not have a coronary care unit and they transferred me to a facility on the North side of Ft. Myers for proper care. Once I was at the new hospital I called my cousin Tim in Chicago, told him I had a heart attack and I was giving him the authority to make medical decisions for me if I was unable to, he was there the next day. I called my ex-wife Debbie, in Tennessee and she and her Father were on their way to Florida.

I woke the next morning to find my cousin Tim, my ex-wife, Debbie and my x-father-in-law and the DCFS case worker all in the room. My Physician came in and suggested they do a heart catheterization on me to look at the heart and see where the blockage was. The case worker told us that Antonio and Angelina would return to foster care. They would not give custody to my ex-wife unless she returned to Florida which she would not do.

Through the next few hours of negotiation we were able to come to a solution. DCFS agreed to give custody to my ex-wife in Tennessee if she would agree that Florida doesn't hold any financial or legal responsibility for the children. I would need to go to court to release custody of the children into Debbie's custody. But, in the best interest of Antonio and Angelina this decision was made although it was a painful decision to come to. I was accustomed to being a Dad again and now they are going to be hundreds of miles away. So the following day my doctors agreed to allow me to leave the hospital to go to court which we did and immediately following the proceeding she left for Tennessee with the children and I was readmitted to the hospital and had the required procedure.

I was recovering from the minor heart attack, Tim returned to Chicago about a week later and I returned to my job. Life went on and I felt the loss of the kid's every day. I got used to having them there and being a Dad.

Donna and I kept in touch even though the kids were gone and when I could get away, I started to visit her in Michigan on weekends. After a couple of months of weekend visits we talked and we decided that I should consider moving up to Michigan and see if we could move our relationship further along. I agreed to come up and see if I could find a job and see how it will go but as a safety measure I would maintain my apartment in Ft. Myers. I loved living in Florida and I really didn't have much desire to move back to the Midwest. But as the old saying goes, everything happens for a reason. Which, I will prove in just a bit.

I packed up my car and drove back to Michigan. I moved to Royal Oak in mid-July of 2005. At the end of July I was offered a position at a mortgage company and started training to sell mortgages. The job was a sales position but with a new twist for me, it was selling mortgages over the telephone. You never met with a client face to face.

Everything was going well and seemed just fine until two weeks into the new job. It was a long day and I was a bit agitated at the end of the day. It was August 15, 2005 at 8:45 PM when my life takes a drastic and highly unexpected turn. This detour would affect many aspects of my life and I never saw it coming.

5

The Mind is a Complicated Computer

In the Detroit area in mid-August they have what is called the 'Dream Cruise'. It is the largest car show in the United States and more than one million people flock to this area for the event. Steve and Evelyn (Donna's parents) lived a block off the main strip, Woodward Ave. Donna and her son went over to their house to sit and watch the hot rods cruise Woodward Ave. while I was at work. I started about eight in the morning and it was about eight in the evening when my shift ended. I wasn't feeling well and was in a bit of a foul mood and I called her and told her I was going back to the apartment. I thought I ate something bad at lunch but told her I would relax a bit, change and come over there. Her parents lived about 3 miles from where we lived.

I arrived home and changed into a T-Shirt and shorts. I had what I thought was the worst case of heartburn I have ever felt. I just couldn't get rid of that feeling. I suddenly started to have shortness of breath. I called her and told her she needed to get home, I didn't know what was wrong but something was not right. She said for me to call 911 but I didn't feel that was necessary and boy was I wrong. I kept tugging on the collar of my T-Shirt to try and breathe easier. It was getting worse and now I felt nausea coming on. It was all evolving so quickly. I put the cell phone on the coffee table and I rushed into the bathroom and when I vomited, it was clear bile. I thought that was peculiar. Once again clear bile came rushing out; over and over, nothing but clear bile.

Then it hit full force, I got weak, felt pain on my left side and collapsed on the floor. I was unable to move, my cellular phone wasn't close to me and I knew at that moment what was happening. I was in serious trouble and I didn't have any control of my destiny and I was at the mercy of GOD's will.

I was having a heart attack. I was laying there on the bathroom floor staring at the toilet and hoping she took me serious enough to be on her way home. I suppose in every tragedy there always is a little comedy. As I lay there, I kept saying to myself that I wasn't going to die looking at a toilet. I could only imagine my Father dying in the same fashion. He went into the bathroom in 1977 and never came out alive. Did he say the same thing? This was a strange coincidence; my Father died in the bathroom and now so will I? I am 47; he was 58, do I win? Is there a prize?

I thought looking at a toilet of all things is a strange way to die. I realize these are obscure things to be thinking about when you are having a heart attack but, the mind is a complicated computer.

As I lay there with bile spilling out of my mouth I kept repeating to myself that I am not going to die looking at a toilet, I am not going to die looking at a toilet, I am not going to die looking at a toilet. Donna and her father Steve arrived and Steve found me on the bathroom floor and she called 911. When she walked into the bathroom she told me the paramedics were on the way, I remember looking at her and saying "good you're here, I am tired, and I am going to sleep now." There is a reason for everything as I mentioned earlier. Perhaps if I was in Florida instead of Michigan, I would not have made it. What I thought was sleep was something completely different. My transition was starting for my journey to the other-side; it was my time to go home.

The Transition to the Afterlife

When I passed over the first time and began my journey to Heaven I remember entering a cloud like tunnel. The tunnel wasn't going straight up; it was more like going into a parallel universe. I was slowly moving through the tunnel and it was bright and it appeared that there were shadows of tree branches surrounding the tunnel. The feelings I experienced were not exactly earthly and they were much more intense.

The first feeling was of peace. It was so calm and serene with an incredible amount of tranquility. All of my Earthly worries, thoughts, fears, opinions, were gone. The intensity of the tranquility was so incredible and overwhelming that there was no fear in what I was experiencing and no fear on where I was going and what to expect when I arrived there.

Then there was warmth. It was as if I was wrapped in a blanket that came out of an oven. It wasn't too hot or too cold, it was simply perfect. It was as if I was in the arms of Angels being held and comforted and carried into Heaven.

Then there was the love. This is a very difficult feeling to describe. Try to remember the first time you saw your child or met your significant other. You know what I am talking about that feeling of first time love that is so positive and so powerful. Now take that feeling and multiply it thousands of times.

Then there was the desire to be home, not at my earthly house but home in Heaven. It was overwhelming. The desire to be home with all of my loved ones and with GOD was like a massive force pulling you toward it and you can't get away even if you wanted to, which you didn't. You wanted to go and be in the glory of GOD and to be with all those that have passed before you.

I was on the way home to where I belong and where I came from. My soul was now free from this earthly bond and traveling back from this journey of knowledge here on earth. The intensity of the feelings were overflowing through me. It is hard to describe the magnitude of it all, but your faith and you're your belief in God suddenly takes over.

I soon came to realize that this was the power of GOD that I was feeling and the love, warmth, peace and tranquility was also caused by the shadows that were surrounding the tunnel. What I thought were tree branches, were not tree branches at all. They were the ones that I loved that have passed before me. They were surrounding the tunnel and holding me and guiding me and welcoming me home. I was so content and so complete and had the most incredible combination of feelings one could ever imagine.

❧

Then in one moment it all stopped and I felt as if someone had grabbed me and was pulling backwards out of the tunnel. I felt as if I was fighting to stop myself from being pulled out and I wanted to continue forward but that wasn't meant to be. It didn't matter how much I struggled, I couldn't continue on, now fear set in. There was mass confusion; I couldn't stop what was happening to my soul. I wanted to go back to the warmth but all the feelings I had were leaving me. They were being drained from me.

The Royal Oak Fire Department Paramedics arrived on scene and resuscitated me. I remember laying there with pain in my chest. Then I recall being in the arms of a fireman and being rushed to the ambulance.

I recall laying on the gurney in the back of the ambulance staring at the light on the ceiling. I felt the IV going into my veins and I hear the call to the hospital. "47 year old male, myocardial infarction resuscitated, ETA 3 minutes."

I don't remember arriving at the hospital or being wheeled into the hospital emergency room. I do not remember the staff working on me. What I do recall is being in the upper corner of the emergency room suite looking down upon my body as approximately twenty people were diligently working to save my life.

I don't remember seeing the faces of the emergency room personnel just their scrubs and white coats. I recall looking down for a while as they frantically worked to revive me. Suddenly I just knew it was time to go and I turned and left. I immediately returned to the tunnel with its warmth and glory and peace and calmness.

The light was getting brighter the closer I got to being home. I remember reaching the end and immediately being embraced with a tremendous feeling of security and safety. My vision was blurred from the light, there was some confusion but the smells were the first of the senses to kick in. I was surrounded by fragrantly sweet scents. It was kind of like the scents of all varieties of all the flowers all in one place. A gentle warm breeze was flowing over me, it was shear perfection. As my vision began to clear, I saw numerous faces all happy and smiling. It felt as if I was being held by so many different souls. Each of which was welcoming me back home. It was difficult to recognize who they were; they were all young as if in their twenties' or early thirties'. But, their faces started to become familiar once again. I knew who they were and the level of happiness that was felt can't be explained in earthly terms. I knew I was safe and I was meant to be there. Off in the distance I saw incredible towers and buildings all glistening with inviting colors. The buildings were familiar but also new to me at the same time. I felt content where I was at and in no hurry to explore. I knew I could visit them soon enough. There is no need to hurry, there is no time. You are just there in an infinite zone to move as you please. I was just glad to be home and surrounded by my loved ones. It felt so right and so normal.

There was a slight bit of confusion and I believe that is caused by the transition. Your soul was leaving your earthly surroundings and now you were in heaven, in the glory of GOD. Those two worlds are never meant to be combined.

It felt as if your soul needs to go through a process of orientation back into Heaven. I think that would have been the next step, looking at your journey to earth and to view all that you have done and to see if you completed the task you were sent to do.

I believe once you get your soul reestablished in Heaven then perhaps you can remember your loved ones on earth and check in on them now and again. But your focus isn't on being on earth; it is there in the Glory of GOD.

I do believe that our souls must learn multiple lessons to grow into more glorious beings and I believe we are sent to earth to learn specific lessons. Whether we learn that lesson or not is because of the free will that we have on earth. The interactions with others can and often do alter your path. Have you ever met someone and thought to yourself, I met this person before but I can't remember where. Then you two will banter back and forth trying to find the common denominator of where you met and the conversation ultimately ends with, "oh well, I don't know but it is strange, isn't it?" I believe you had met before and that soul had such a profound effect on yours in a previous life that you remembered it. The magical thing about this is your time on earth doesn't allow you to maintain your memories of past adventures and the lessons you were here to learn.

Have you ever met a child or a younger person and they seemed so much more mature for their particular age? Or have you met someone that acted much younger than their earthly years? I believe that is the age of their soul coming through. This gives us a small window into their souls and the lessons they have learned.

The more mature is a more advanced soul and the other is a younger soul in its lessons and journeys. Since there is no time in Heaven our soul can remain there indefinitely or we can chose to return and take on new lessons that will ultimately bring us closer to GODLINESS. Then it happened again...............

❧

I once again felt the pull back out of Heaven. I felt that I was fighting hard not to leave this glorious place that I was in. I fought but to no avail, I was returning to earth but I wanted to know why I had to leave and why I couldn't stay, but I received no answers.

The next thing that happened was even stranger. I suddenly sat up. My girlfriend was in a chair next to the bed; her head was resting on the mattress. I woke her and asked what was happening and where we were at and what time it was. She looked at me as if she saw a ghost and ran out of the room and returned with a nurse. A doctor arrived and they began to check me over. It all seemed like a blur. So many people were converging on me at once. After things calmed down in my room, I asked what all the commotion was about.

I found out that I was in a coma for four days!

Within a few days I was released from the hospital with a full beard and 20 pounds lighter. The medical quest now started to find out the causes of this deadly enigma in my chest. The Doctor gave me a copy of the picture of the arteries in my heart and circled the 'one' in pen that was closed off and caused the cardiac arrest. The first question; was the artery stented and reopened? The response was not what I wanted to hear. The artery was too small and narrow to stent. They felt the best option at this time is to medically treat the body.

This was an unnerving feeling to know that I had a blocked artery in my heart and they couldn't fix it. I was walking around just waiting for it to react again.

I was assured the medications would help in my recovery. The medication run then started. Cartia XT to relax the heart, Plavix to thin the blood, Aspirin to help prevent another cardiac arrest, Lipitor to lower and control the cholesterol and there were a few others.

It seemed like a full court press in medication to see what would work. Lipitor has a warning that goes "If you take Lipitor (atorvastatin calcium) tablets, tell your doctor if you feel any new muscle pain or weakness. This could be a sign of rare but serious muscle side effects."

Yes, I had that but I didn't know it at that time. Driving home was a chore because I couldn't hold the steering wheel because pain was too great and I had to steer with one finger. Turning a door knob would cause terribly intense pain. Getting undressed or going to the bathroom was extremely painful. I had to sleep on the couch and be wrapped tightly in a blanket so I wouldn't move because every movement caused more pain. This went on for weeks. My Doctors didn't know why this was happening.

Work became more and more difficult to perform or even get too. I couldn't raise my arms or even hold a pen without pain. One evening I woke in the middle of the night to use the bathroom. I used my thumbs to pull down my sweat pants and the pain was so horrific I had a syncope episode fell into the bathroom door knocked myself out cold and they had to remove me from the apartment in an ambulance. Finally they admitted it was the Lipitor and immediately removed me from that drug.

Getting the proper doses of the medication dialed in was time consuming. It was difficult not only physically but mentally. I never knew what side-affect would occur next. Over the next three years I had at least six hospital visits for drug reactions and additional Angina attacks.

It all FINALLY got dialed in and I found even ground to walk on. Now I could concentrate on my mental recovery. The mind is a complicated computer.

6

Is This Really Happening?

I had to make a decision to return to Florida or to stay in Michigan. From a medical perspective, I decided I needed to stay in Michigan. I made arrangements for myself, Donna and one of her girlfriends to fly to Ft. Myers. I rented a U-Haul and a rental car and the plan was to load the U-Haul with the furnishings from the apartment, then we would get a hotel on Ft. Myers beach and the following day they would drive the truck up to Michigan and in a couple of days I would fly back. We arrived in Florida on a Friday and I was to fly out on Monday. We got the truck loaded and checked into this little motel on Ft. Myers beach. It was a small place with maybe 15 rooms and it was beachfront on the Gulf of Mexico. We went and had dinner, enjoyed the ocean air, the tropical like atmosphere and some music and then returned to the motel. The next morning we got up and laid out on the beach to get a little sun tan before they started their drive back to Michigan. As we lay there, there was a storm brewing out in the Gulf of Mexico. It was very far offshore and the clouds were black and ominous. The sun was still bright and warm on the beach where we were at. I went in to the room, which was ground level and about 35 yards from the ocean's edge, and turned on the weather channel to see what was going on in the Gulf. It was Hurricane Katrina that just passed by the Florida Keys on its way to its final destination that was targeted as the Louisiana coast. I returned to the beach and told the girls what they were seeing out there.

I had lived in Florida on two separate occasions. I just went through the 2004 Florida hurricane season of Charley, Ivan, Frances and Jeanne that crisscrossed the state.

Back in 1977, while I was in the U.S. Navy, I also went through Hurricane Babe while living in the Florida Panhandle. I wasn't a novice to Florida hurricanes, I been through 5 hurricanes and survived them all.

The good news was Katrina was well off shore and it was tracking toward the Louisiana coast. We enjoyed the next few hours before they decided that they should leave. It was over a twenty four hour drive back to Michigan. So, at approximately two in the afternoon they got on the road.

I returned to the beach and this was the first time since I was discharged from the hospital that I felt calm, comfortable and content. The solitude of being by myself for the first time in quite a while, gave me a sense of satisfaction. I loved being on the beach with the sand in between my toes, the salt air smell and the warm Florida sun caressing my body. It was a moment of true happiness, although I was sad at the same time, because I was going to miss living there. Florida was home to me, I loved Florida and what it had to offer. I did my Navy boot camp in Orlando, I was in a helicopter squadron in the panhandle and I spent time on the USS Lexington in Pensacola Naval Base and of course my recent time is S.W. Florida.

As I laid there with the sun caressing my face, I felt a few drops of rain. The ominous black clouds of Katrina seemed to be getting closer. The ocean picked up a bit but nothing to be alarmed about, after all this wasn't my first hurricane. The sun started to fade to grey and the rain started to fall harder. I went in and tuned into the weather channel to insure that Katrina didn't decide to take a right turn and was coming our way. The surf was getting stronger the wind started to howl louder. The weather people were saying it appeared Katrina may be taking a turn toward Southern Florida but they were hoping it would track back out to sea.

I could hear the rain pounding against the side of the building. I looked out the window facing the ocean and I could see the waves rolling in with much more force and taking over the beach.

We still had power so I sat back on the sofa and I was glued to the T.V. As I sat there I started to hear a dripping sound. I looked at the two windows facing the ocean and water was coming into the room through the window seams. Water was also coming in under the front door. I grabbed towels from the bathroom as well as the area rug and tried to block the water coming in under the doorway.

I opened the window blinds and the ocean was starting to get as high as the window. I was slowly realizing that escape was non-existent. I went into the kitchen hoping I would be able to get out through the small kitchen window but the water surrounded the building and my rental car had water climbing up its doors. Water was still leaking in through the window seams and the towels at the door were getting saturated. I grabbed all the bed linens in the room and used them to soak up as much water as I could.

I looked out the window again that was facing Katrina and she was angry and the water was climbing higher up the window. I was in disbelief. I just stood there in ankle deep water in my motel room for what seemed like hours. I was looking at my sixth Hurricane; I was just released from the hospital after having a cardiac arrest. I died, went to the Heaven, was still in disbelief about that and I came back all to die again by a hurricane in a hotel room alone in Ft. Myers? I thought GOD had a horrible sense of humor to allow this to be happening.

You begin to question GODs reasoning and ask why he does things like this. I had no options, no way of escape from this room, at the time the windows and the door were holding the water back from completely flooding the room. All I could do was to grab my small travel bag climb on top of the kitchen counter and then on top of the refrigerator and wait for Katrina to take me.

As I sat there, my mind was traveling at the speed of sound in so many directions. I tried to make a few cellular calls but there was no service, there was no one I could call for help or I could call to say goodbye too.

Minutes turned into hours as the water continued to make its way into the room. The wind was howling through the palm trees and past the buildings. You could hear the ocean slapping up against the building. Time slowed down as if you could hear each tick of the clock.

The floor had about 8-10 inches of water covering it and climbing, water was still seeping in through the window seams, the towels and linens and the area rug were soaked thoroughly and were useless.

It was nothing but a matter of time at this point. I was waiting for the windows to break and the waters of the Gulf of Mexico to flood the room. Then as suddenly as it came, it seemed to leave. The wind died down and an eerie calm was heard outside. The sun started to peak through the clouds and I got off of the refrigerator and waded through the calf deep water in my room to the window. I was thinking we were in the eye of the hurricane which is normally calm before the second wave of wind, rain and storm surge arrive. It didn't make sense to climb out of the kitchen window to escape the room because there was nowhere else for me to go. I thought about going to the back side of the building and get myself to the 2nd floor but changed my mind. If this was the eye and I left the room I would be caught outside when the second wave hit and that would be deadly. So my best option was to wait it out in the room I was in.

It took a good couple of hours but the water began to recede. About eight PM I was able to open the door to the room and walk outside to see the damage that was left behind. Sand was everywhere, seaweed and palm tree branches were strewn about. My rent-a-car was flooded and I opened the door to empty it out. The lounge chairs that were on the beach were all over the property and on the other side of the road of the motel. The sun started to break through the clouds as Katrina made her way to New Orleans and we unfortunately know how that turned out. I survived my sixth hurricane.

I grabbed my things waited for a while for a car or taxi to pass by so I could get inland. I eventually found a ride and went to a hotel near the airport where I could dry out, take a hot shower and wake the next morning to fly back to Michigan.

⧡⧡

After my return to Michigan, my depression continued to worsen and the final straw came a few days after my return. My girlfriend ended the relationship because she couldn't take all the medical challenges that I was facing. I couldn't be angry with her, it was difficult for me to deal with the things that were happening to me and she had a 2 year old to care for, and it was a heavy load for her to carry. This happened right at the time that I was getting ready to close on a condominium I bought for us to live in. The questions started over again, should I just cancel the deal, should I go back to Florida? Should I go back to Arizona, Las Vegas or back to Chicago? I decided to stay in Michigan because I felt that they had the best knowledge on my medical situation. At least I had a job to keep me occupied and income coming in.

The Angina attacks started to become more frequent. It was November 2007; I went to work and the very first thing two female co-workers said to me, was, "you look horrible". Well, good morning to you too! They talked me into going to the hospital to get checked out and drove me there. I began to have chest pains and my thoughts went to heart attack.

As I lay on the gurney, I felt the left side of my body become numb and the left side of my face also went numb and felt tingly. I told the nurse and she immediately contacted my Cardiologist and they decided to go in and check the heart for blockage once again.

Once the procedure was completed and I lay in the recovery room, my cardiologist came in to review his findings.

He felt the numbness was caused by a Transient Ischemic Attack (T.I.A.) a mini stroke that can last for minutes to twenty four hours and then clears itself. It is a serious event since it is a precursor to a full blown stroke but, it is manageable. My cardiologist then diagnosed me with Vaso Spasmatic Angina. The medical definition is; "Coronary artery spasm is a temporary, sudden narrowing of one of the coronary arteries (the arteries that supply blood to the heart). The spasm slows or stops blood flow through the artery and starves part of the heart of oxygen-rich blood. Spasm may be "silent" -- without symptoms -- or it may result in chest pain or angina. If the spasm lasts long enough, it may even cause a heart attack."

He said when he looked at the heart and specifically the artery that was originally shut down in 2005; he found it to be open and working well. That is how he came to the conclusion of the diagnosis as Vaso Spasmatic Angina.

Now I want you to imagine what this means, open your mind's eye and think about it. At any time, an artery in the heart can collapse and shut down and if it doesn't open quickly the lack of blood flow can cause cardiac arrest. That is a very heavy burden to be carrying around on a daily basis. I have had other attacks and a nitro glycerin pill has opened the artery(s). The constant fear is always there. I have to keep it out of my mind or I would be crippled with fear and never leave my home.

After this diagnosis, I told myself to live life, I force myself to do what I want to, but all the while I maintain what may happen in the back of my mind and I always carry nitro glycerin pills with me.

This entire experience separated me mentally. On one side I was working, doing my job, making money. I had friends at work and a social life. On the other side I was mentally challenged by my experience and was struggling to understand the reality of my transition to Heaven.

Some people were skeptical with my "death" experience, how can you blame them? I was skeptical also, but I also knew what had happened and what I did experience. How can these things be explained? I began a path of understanding and investigation. I read about others and their "near death experiences", I also read up on the scientific studies and what the scientific community thought of NDE's. (This will be reviewed later in this book)

People often said to me, why are you depressed? You are alive, you're here! I can accept people's skepticism but until you have actually crossed the line from the living to the dead, then you have no concept of how this feels or how this affects you when and if you return. People always say I almost died. Pick up any People magazine and at any given moment there is some star saying I almost died but I beat cancer, or, I beat my drug addiction or I would have died if I fell off the horse on a movie shoot or I almost died because one of my red MM's got stuck in my throat and one of my 47 member entourage saved me from choking to death, or a variety of other examples.

One can say I almost died when I was very ill or I almost died when I was in that car accident. All are horrible things to go through but almost is not the same as did. I feel for the pain they suffered and I empathize with their experience but the fact is your heart did not stop and you did not take a last breath of life. There is a difference.

People also call this a "near death" experience. I am not fond of that label. Calling it that is like saying a girl is "near pregnant". What I experienced was not a "near death" experience, (nor was I near pregnant); it was a "DEATH" experience. This label needs to take over for these types of experiences. Perhaps this book will help promote this change and open the minds of the skeptics.

A Message on Cancer

I truly feel for those that are battling cancer, and I do not disparage their situation. I would not and do not want to face that fight.

It is a disturbing thought to think that something is destroying your body from the inside and you have to go through Hell to try and save your life. It is a life altering experience and that changes you medically and mentally. I have also lost some friends to this dreaded disease and I have seen the toll it can take on one's body and mind. I also saw how it affects those that are left behind, the dreaded 'C' word is far reaching, and the survivors must be strong. It is a difficult battle and all those that are in that fight, keep on fighting and never give up. Don't let the bastard (death) get you, fight hard to live another day!

But, if that time does come and you realize that you can no longer fight off the scourge within your body, find peace within yourself. I know it is easy for me to say, "Don't be afraid". Death is something we all fear. It is the finality of your life here on earth but the continuation of your bigger life, the advancement of your soul.

Please know that there is a wonderful place and loving souls anxiously awaiting your return home. Please know that you will be terribly missed here on earth but those that are left behind will be OK and their lives will go forward. I know it is difficult, but know that you can go in peace.

May GOD be with you, watch over you and help you in your fight for life. May you be as pain free as possible and may your focus stay positive.

7

Cemeteries and Burials

I was feeling so many different things. I was depressed on how my personal life had turned out, I was depressed because of the way I was feeling, I was depressed that I couldn't push myself harder at work and I was depressed that I was in a new area and my family wasn't there for support. I then found myself being depressed because I was alive. I could not shake how good being back in Heaven felt. I would relive the feelings I had that day of August 15, 2005; those incredible feelings of calm and peace, of warmth and compassion and the feeling of unconditional love. I wanted to feel that again and the fact that I couldn't feel it gnawed at me daily. The movie projector in my mind played it over and over again.

The next year or two was up and down, I tried my best to keep my mind occupied and tried so hard not to think of those days in August. I dated on and off but nothing serious. Then I met someone; I met Lisa and she was the one for me. Lisa is a teacher of Art at a local school district and she was also Italian. We were married on May 30th 2009. I told her about what I went through and how I felt. She knew where I was mentally but I don't believe she knew how deeply this was affecting me. She suggested I talk to someone and I have to admit, she made sense. As it turns out, some 5 years later, she always makes sense. She is always right, even when I think she is wrong!

I want to make this clear; I was not suicidal. I was simply disappointed to be here. My life as I knew it and wanted it had taken a dramatic turn. Lisa was now the bright light in this dark space. I decided to see a Psychologist to try and work through these feeling.

I was still in the mortgage business and I was getting more disenfranchised with it. The mortgage industry was taking a severe downturn in 2007 and 2008. My financial situation was critical and since the downturn was so quick and so dramatic, my income was greatly affected. I decided to leave my company and take a job with a Cadillac franchise. It was a way to earn money quickly to be able to maintain my financial position. That went well for a while until General Motors filed for a bankruptcy and our business dropped off significantly resulting in four of us being laid off.

While I was still dealing with my other demons I made the decision to join a local Cemetery Group helping the survivors take care of their loved ones and helping them plan for the inevitable. Somehow I thought this may be good therapy for me in addition to speaking with a therapist. I found this job to be exactly what I hoped it would be. It was another part of my spiritual journey to find the answers I sought.

I was close to death every day. I helped people dealing with the ones they lost and by doing this it brought me closure. I attended between three and six funerals a week. I learned how the physical aspect of death worked. I learned of the various burial options. I learned how different families and individuals deal with death. It was quite interesting to see these variations. It was also interesting to see how the different religions deal with death and burials.

I have always had a Gothic sort of attraction to cemeteries. When I was a young boy we would visit Queen of Heaven Cemetery in suburban Hillside Illinois and visit our relatives. I always had an attraction to that place and also to Mt. Carmel Cemetery across Roosevelt Rd. The history and the stories these particular cemeteries tell are amazing. The mausoleum at Queen of Heaven is enormous and holds over 30,000 souls in one building.

To some, cemeteries are taboo, or scary or too final. Some people can't face the fact that we will all die. Some people ignore the reality of death while in life. I, on the other hand, find a cemetery a peaceful area filled with history, architecture, solace and love. A cemetery isn't the end of life it is the continuance of your soul. Perhaps if people will view the cemetery for what it is, then perhaps their fear of death will also fade away.

The next time you are in a cemetery, look past the death and see the life. The monuments tell so many stories and give us so much history of all that are interred there. We all have value here on earth regardless of our social status. We all have a history and we all have a genealogy. A cemetery is history and all it truly takes is to open your eyes and see what it is all about.

When I travel I do enjoy visiting local graveyards. There are always different styles, the peacefulness and quiet of the location and the architecture of the private mausoleums and the different styles of the headstones and monuments vary as much as their individual locations. A couple of my favorite Cemeteries are Lafayette Cemetery in New Orleans, Woodlawn Cemetery in Detroit and the cemetery in Key West. The Key West City Cemetery was established in 1847 following a hurricane in 1846. The original cemetery was a beachside cemetery and due to the winds and storm surge it unearthed the graves. The cemetery was then moved to its current location and the Key West cemetery is still active with about 100 interments a year. It is estimated that 80,000-100,000 souls are interred there.

Lafayette Cemetery in NOLA dates back to the 1800's and was originally part of a planation. Because of the water table in NOLA, the vast majority of the graves are above ground free standing private mausoleums and vaults in the wall surrounding the cemetery. Woodlawn in Detroit has some of the most fascinating private mausoleum of the automotive industries founding fathers. All three are worth the visit.

With my experience in the funeral business, it opened up my desire for knowledge as to what happens to the human body when we die. I researched and learned and I feel it is something that we need to understand because it is part of life and indeed part of our spirituality.

We must accept what the inevitable will be and decide how we wish to spend eternity in our earthly form.

For an in-ground burial, a burial vault is necessary and they come in a variety of options. All cemeteries will require the use of a vault/ liner for the casket to be placed into. A vault will stop the ground from dropping from the weight of equipment and the natural erosion and eventual collapse of the coffin. Vaults also help protect the casket and the remains from water, moisture, and insects and will slow the decomposition process. They come in various costs and styles. The basic, least expensive vault is made of concrete and is not lined. The next upgrade will be lined and also have a sealed lip to give additional help in the resistance of moisture, water and bugs. The vault is lined with a waterproof material similar to the material that is used on the foundation of a house. Then you can get some with a plastic liner or you can really step up and spend some money. You can get a copper or bronze vault. They will last longer and be stronger. The goal of a vault is to preserve the body longer, and not allow the ground around the coffin to erode. But the decomposition process will not be stopped. You can also place a flat granite marker to mark the grave or you can be more elaborate and mark the grave with larger upright monuments.

The next option is placement in a mausoleum. This is the most expensive of the three options mentioned here. A mausoleum is designed like a honeycomb. Crypts can be a single, head to toe for two or side by side for two. The mausoleum crypt itself acts as the burial vault.

The coffin is then placed into the crypt and a concrete panel is placed over the opening of the vault and then a marble cover with the name and date of birth and date of death of the deceased on the outside. These will stay dry and mostly bug free.

The third option and least expensive option is cremation. Cremation is becoming more popular with the rising costs of funeral services and burial options. The funeral director will remove any items not wished to be cremated along with the body. If the deceased had a pacemaker or other type of implanted medical device, it too will need to be removed to prevent an explosion from occurring during the cremation process. It is not necessary to embalm a body before the cremation unless the family wishes to have a public viewing of the body during a memorial service.

The body is then placed in a cremation casket, usually made of wood, or more often a cremation container which is basically a large cardboard box with a plywood bottom for sturdiness. These types of containers will burn well during the cremation cycle. The casket is then placed in the cremation chamber. Temperatures within the chamber often reach the 1800°F - 2000°F range. The burners within a cremator are fueled by either natural gas or propane. It generally takes about two to three hours for a body to be completely reduced to just the bone fragments by cremation.

Once cremated the remains are placed in an urn. The family will have a multitude of urn options. The urn can then be placed in a cremation crypt at the cemetery, it can be placed in the ground in a burial plot or the family can keep the remains at home. Cremation options are getting more creative.

There are a few companies that specialize in placing the remains in a under the sea burial site. The remains are mixed with concrete into a form to make a swim through reef. It is marked with a plate with the deceased name and year of birth and date of death.

One company has built a roman style underwater cemetery with tremendous options off the coast of Florida. It is well worth a look if that option interests you.

The Breakdown of the Body

I will keep this part fairly basic; four paragraphs should be enough information. Whether you prefer an in-ground burial, or a mausoleum burial, the body itself will go through a normal decomposition process.

Human decomposition begins approximately four minutes after death has occurred. Once there is no oxygen supplying the cells of the body, the cells begin to dissolve from the inside out, eventually causing them to rupture, and releasing nutrient-rich fluids. This process begins and progresses more rapidly in tissues that have high enzyme content (such as the liver) and high water content such as the brain.

The blood in the body will settle causing discoloration of the skin and cellular cytoplasm (The cytoplasm is the gel-like substance residing within the cell membrane holding all of the cell's internal sub-structures) has gelled due to rigor mortis. After enough cells have ruptured, nutrient-rich fluids become available and the process of putrefaction can begin. Putrefaction is the destruction of the soft tissues of the body by the action of micro-organisms and results in the catabolism of tissue into gases, liquids and simple molecules. Shortly after the purging of gases due to putrefaction, active decay of the remains will begin.

Contrary to popular belief, embalming of the body does not preserve the body forever; it just delays the inevitable process of decomposition. There are variations in the rate of decomposition based on the strength of the chemicals and methods used when the body was embalmed, and the humidity and temperature of the burial of choice whether it be in-ground or mausoleum.

Embalming can preserve a body, so that it remains recognizable several months after death, but typically within a year, the tissue is mostly gone and bones and teeth are usually all that is left.

The Act of Burial

The families I have dealt with were as diverse as the burial products that are available. I have seen acts of love and sadness that I can never imagine how much pain they felt. I have seen the opposite as if the death, the wake and burial were nothing more than an inconvenience.

I want to give you examples of both. There will be no names given, but after you read this I would like you to stop and think to yourself how you will handle the loss of your loved one and ask yourself; what will I do when _____ passes on?

Part of my position at the cemetery was to sell memorials; granite and marble headstones, memorial benches, flat markers, vaults, plots and mausoleum spaces. Some of the stories I would listen too were truly heartbreaking. You felt the pain the family was feeling and you felt the love they have for the deceased, you found yourself trying to find a way to memorialize their loved one as economically and as grand as possible.

One of my favorite functions was actually doing a unique design to help memorialize their loved one. I could take a generic memorial bench and turn it into a family memory, or do the same with a headstone. I feel the families appreciated what I was trying to accomplish for them.

This first one had a lot of meaning for me. It was the grave of a young man of no more than seventeen years of age. He was hit by a train. I would drive through the cemetery and I always saw flowers and balloons at his grave site. The family had a nice flat bronze memorial head stone of him playing hockey and a nice picture of him all in color. It was a beautiful marker but it couldn't be seen unless you walked up to it. I saw the love and without even talking to them, I also saw the pain they felt by what they would leave at his grave. I looked up who the family was and without talking to them I designed a beautiful Memorial Bench with the bronze colored plaque of their son mounted upright and two flower vases on each side of the bench. I called the family and asked if I could stop by.

They allowed me into their home and I presented what I had designed. They were shocked that I would do this for them without being asked. They couldn't afford what I had put together but they did have the Bronze colored plaque with his picture and a picture of him playing hockey placed on a piece of upright granite and it serves the exact same purpose. They have a memorial they can see from the road it is a great memory of their lost son.

Another was a family who also lost their son. He was in his twenties and he was a newspaper reporter. They already had a beautiful memorial placed for their only son. I offered them a custom bench with his picture on it, and it listed his fraternities and his history of accomplishments. I visited with them many times just to chat. They were a fantastic family and their loss carried tremendous pain.

One of my most memorable of families lost their Patriarch. They were musicians and the family was very close. I designed a bench for his wife that she could sit on and visit him. On the backside of the stand we listed all his grandchildren. On the front we had a violin carved into the granite, and pictures of him. I had a new employee trainee with me that day.

The graveside service was large. It seemed as if the entire family was there, people of all ages. A nephew played his guitar and sang many songs after the minister said his final words. Once we were set for the burial itself we called in the grounds crew that lowered his coffin into the vault and the backhoe covered the grave back in. The family didn't leave for quite a while.

They stayed and played and sang numerous songs. We stayed with them. After about another hour or so his wife came up to me and said that I had to come with them to the luncheon. She was so appreciative of what we did for their family. I respectfully declined their invitation; I had another funeral scheduled that day.

Once we left the new employee asked me how long I had known that family. I told her, since yesterday. You get close to families very quickly in situations like this.

⚬⚬⚬

On the other side there are families that are still very nice but the funeral is nothing more than something they had to do. You still gain a good rapport with these families but how they handle this business is often very different from what was described above.

One family lost their Father. There was no funeral home visitation, they had a sole hearse deliver the casket which was actually a cremation wood box which we placed in the base level vault and placed him in the ground without any family present and without a marker for the burial.

A families Mother had passed away. She had three sons. Two who were not financially sound and one that was. This was one of my first funerals. There was no doubt they loved their Mother. They had a service for her in our Mausoleum and she had pre-purchased a plot.

Typically the hearse will pull up in front of the Mausoleum and the pall bearers would bring the casket into entry way. It would be placed on a low gurney and wheeled to the front of the chapel. Once the service was completed, the casket would be rolled to the entrance and the pall bearers would return the casket to the hearse and a procession would take place from the Chapel to the grave site. This was a new experience for me on this particular funeral.

We had the family and friends that were present leave the chapel and return to their vehicles. Once the chapel was clear, we rolled the casket to the back door of the mausoleum. My supervisor arrived and two gentlemen came in and opened the casket. They knew my supervisor and were having a basic conversation like they were at the bar. I found out as I watched that the casket was a rental casket! You learn something new every day.

The deceased was in a plastic box and they slid her out of the end of the coffin and placed the lid on the plastic box and placed it in our onsite hearse. Our hearse then went to the grave site and they placed the box into a basic vault and continued with the completion of the burial.

Of course, as in any other business, strange things happen in the funeral business also. One of the strangest things I did witness was a mausoleum burial. The crypt was at the 'Heaven' level which is the top level in this outdoor mausoleum.

A mechanical lift was needed to raise the casket up to that level and then the casket would be slid into the crypt. The ground crew would throw B.B.'s into the crypt to make the casket tray slide in easier into the honeycombed vault. The casket is then placed into a black plastic tray and the tray has approximately 4 inch high sides. We will not go into the need for this tray.

In the funeral business deceased individuals of certain sizes would need a specialty casket to fit their girth. This was one of those situations.

Unfortunately this information wasn't passed on to the cemetery staff from the funeral home or from the family when the final arrangements were being made at the cemetery. The grounds crew had the casket on the lift. The Family was gathered, some crying, all looking up at the opening of the final resting place of their loved one.

The lift stops at the top level, they spread the B.B.'s into the crypt, and there was one groundkeeper on each side of the casket as they slid it to the opening.

Suddenly they stopped; the casket wouldn't fit into the crypt. The opening of a single crypt is a standard size. The oversized casket would not fit into the opening.

One woman was in tears and in a loud voice she yelled, "Oh my, he doesn't want to go!" We held our composure but it was a bit funny. The solution to this was a total reworking of the burial plans with both the cemetery and the funeral home absorbing most of the additional costs.

Shortly after this last burial, my previous company called and I received an offer to return to the mortgage business on a new team and it was an offer I couldn't refuse. My wife agreed and I started back in November of 2009. My job couldn't have been better. The team I was on was amazing, the income was amazing and many options were opening up internally. After a couple of years the team I was on was dissolved and I decided to get out of the sales side of the business and into the operations end of the business. Once again it was a great move and all was well and life itself was going very well. Lisa and I were solid; we had great friends and a good life.

All good things must come to an end, so the saying goes, and it came to an abrupt halt in April 2012.

8

It Couldn't Happen Twice?

It was October 2011; I just had some minor knee surgery and I was starting a new internal position at work. At our company we always have raffles of some sort or another and this particular raffle was for an all-expense paid trip for two to San Diego for the University of North Carolina and Michigan State University opening day basketball game. Now the game may not sound so terrific and you may ask why it wasn't in Michigan or in North Carolina? It was on the deck of the Aircraft Carrier U.S.S. Carl Vinson CVN-70 at dock at the San Diego Naval Base. President and Michelle Obama also attended the game as well as other dignitaries. The tickets for this event were very limited to U.S. Military personnel and employees of the sponsors of the event. I bought 2 raffle tickets and I was one of the winners. We were off for San Diego in November for this special event.

The trip was incredible and as a U.S. Navy veteran it brought back a lot of pride. The one thing besides this great basketball game in San Diego and being within 40 feet of a sitting President was the U.S.S. Carl Vinson itself. This is the ship that carried the body of Osama Bin Ladin to his final resting place somewhere in the ocean. This was a once in a lifetime experience.

Christmas and New Year's came and went and the harsh mid-west winter was taking its toll. February 2012 was the time for our annual excursion to Mexico and that year's destination was Playa Del Carmen for a week of fun and sun.

In April 2012 the time was here again to start the annual chore of prepping our boat, Nauti Time, a 30' Chris Craft for the upcoming summer on Lake St. Clair.

It was Saturday the 21st of April, and I had to go into the office for about four hours. I was sitting at my desk and all of a sudden I got quite dizzy. I thought it was lack of food so I completed what I had to do and I stopped and grabbed a burger and I felt better. I then went to Nauti Time to do some work that she needed prior to launching. After I was done, I was driving home on the highway when a T.I.A. (Transient Ischemic Attack) hit. I went numb on the left side of my body. My left leg and arm went weak and I called my wife and had her stay on the phone with me until I got home. Once I returned home I tried to eat, I took a shower but I wasn't feeling any better and we made the decision that we should go to the hospital.

What I thought would be a day or two of tests as it always have been turned into a 17 day odyssey that would once again change my life forever.

⧫

I was admitted into the Hospital in Royal Oak, MI. on the 21st of April 2012 with a Transient Ischemic Attack. On Sunday, the 22nd, I passed out in the restroom of my hospital room for an unknown reason and badly bruised the right side of my face swelled my right eye shut and I caused a wound on my forehead. Once they stabilized me and stopped the bleeding from my forehead, they rushed me in for blood tests, Cat Scans, MRI's. The lab reports showed hemoglobin of 13.8, the CAT Scan and MRI's were normal. Over the next few days the syncope episodes continued. My Cardiologist, my Physician Asst. and General Practitioner were perplexed on this sudden turn of new events.

My Cardiology team called in another Cardiology team to confer on these symptoms. On Wednesday the 25th of April they performed what is called a T.E.E procedure to view the back side of my heart. This procedure was done under anesthesia and no labs were pulled for this procedure.

On the 26th of April, The electro-cardiologist, with my Cardiology Team, scheduled a surgery to implant a heart recording device in my chest right above my heart that will record the hearts activities and lock in abnormal rhythms within certain ranges specified by cardiology. The surgery was to take place at approximately 12:30 PM on Friday the 27th of April.

At 8:45 AM on the morning of the 27th the lab report stated my hemoglobin had dropped to 10.7. This was the first hemoglobin check since April 22nd. The normal range for male hemoglobin is a minimum of 13.8 and a maximum of 17.2. The result of a 3.1 drop in Hemoglobin in four days that is clearly marked on the lab report in bold and as 'LOW' was overlooked. The surgery to implant the loop recorder proceeded. There was no hemoglobin check post-surgery and none on the 28th of April (Saturday) the following day.

I anticipated I would return home and recover from the heart recorder surgery on Sunday but those best laid plans were put to rest approximately 3:00 AM on Sunday morning.

(I apologize in advance for some of the graphic detail, but to be fully conscience for this is truly an experience that doesn't occur often)

I woke and reached just a few inches for the urinal on the table next to the bed and suddenly vomited violently then became light headed. It was dark in the room and the bile was just as black. I rang the nurse button and they arrived as I violently vomited again and passed out.

Once I blacked out they called the rapid response team. They brought me back from the darkness, and found my heart rate in the thirties. They stabilized me and decided to move me to a cardiac care room about 5:00 AM. We were able to get Lisa (my wife) to the hospital at about 6:30 AM or 6:45 AM. Life as I knew it went down from there.

There was pain in my stomach that was increasing, my heart rate was volatile and bouncing all around. My blood pressure was also volatile and dropping. Per the lab reports, my hemoglobin was at a level of 4.9 at 4:00 AM before they moved me to critical care. They used an IV that I had in my right arm and replaced a fluid bag with a pint of B+ blood. This wasn't enough. The Physician's Assistant, Ken Jackson, who was on duty (who works for my cardiology team) was working on me and realized I was bleeding out internally and then everything went into high gear. My heart rate and blood pressure was falling.

He ordered the two nurses at my bedside to get additional I.V.s started because they needed to get more blood into me stat. My veins were all collapsing there wasn't a vein that could be used due to the lack of fluid and blood in my body. The Physicians Asst. refused to give up. At that moment, my wife walked into the room to see how I was doing, she said I was shaking and I was grey in color. We heard someone yell for the crash cart. My mind was racing at this point because this is the first time I realized I was in serious trouble. I recall telling the Physician's Assistant, "I am done, I am going" and he responded "You aren't going anywhere today". It was approximately 7:30 AM. When I saw the tunnel that I had been in before open behind him, I knew then, I was close.

The room was frantic with action. The Physician's Assistant had my right hand and was frantically sticking a needle into the top of my hand trying desperately to find a vein so he could add another pint of blood to my body. I didn't feel any pain from being stuck repeatedly with the needle.

I could not be medicated to relieve any pain or stress, my vitals were too weak. I was helpless and at the mercy of GOD and the skills of Mr. Jackson the Physician's Assistant.

My wife was standing there staring in shock as to what was happening in front of her. I looked at Lisa standing there and I remember the fear in her eyes and can only imagine the terror she felt. We hear the nurse stating my heart rate and my blood pressure readings and they were dropping quickly.

The nurse then started the countdown of my life.

"Heart rate falling, 12-11-10-9-8………" Another nurse stepped in and grabbed my wife by the arm and started pulling her out of the room. Our eyes met for what I thought was the very last time as we heard my heart monitor begin the sound of 'flat line'.

All went black, I took my last breath. I had died.

⸎

Once I passed on, my transition to the other-side started again. The amazing thing about this space between life and death and the transition to the other side is there is no aspect of time.

Time is an earthly action. We wake when the sun comes up and we know it is getting late when the sun goes down. We fight time to get to work on schedule and to get home in the evening. We cherish time, it tells us when our children's birthdays are and when it is the holidays such as Christmas and Thanksgiving and Easter. Time tells us when our favorite television show is on or when our home team is playing. Time tells us how long we have been married or how long we have been divorced. Time tells us that twelve million years ago dinosaurs' roamed the earth. Time tells us everything. Time controls all aspects of our 'time' here on earth.

But, when you cross that threshold from the living to the deceased, time becomes non-existent and irrelevant. Back on earth the hospital staff still may be working diligently to resuscitate you. But even the diligent hospital staff, after a set amount of time, will forego their efforts and let you stay in the realm of the deceased.

Since I passed through this threshold not once but twice now I knew what I should have expected. I didn't expect this transition would be different but I must admit that neither transition was the same as the other. I had two totally different experiences. The same thing happened. I was alive and then I wasn't. I ended up in Heaven but in different places with different things happening.

This time I was married to a wonderful woman; I had great friends and my life was on a great path. About 6 months earlier my cousin Tim and I were able to bring our extended family together for the first family reunion in over twenty years.

Through e-mails, Facebook, contact with cousins gathering email addresses and phone numbers we were able to put together a family reunion that went from a small golf outing to a reunion that covered four generations. We ended up with over eighty five people with some coming from Nebraska, Michigan, Tennessee, California, Arizona and Indiana. It was an incredible event and standing there speaking that evening with Tim standing next to me; well, we were both overwhelmed that in a very short amount of time we were able to make this event happen. We brought our family back together and everyone made the effort to be there and make it happen. That was a very powerful evening.

I Didn't Want To Go

When it happened this time I was fighting more to stay here on earth. I remember my apprehension to enter the tunnel. Although I was fighting, my soul knew that the right thing to do was enter the tunnel.

The tunnel was different this time; the shadows surrounding the tunnel weren't there. It was brighter this time and I seemed to be moving faster to the next realm. It also was warmer and seemed even more comforting and more calming.

I once again returned to the other side and the peace and calmness was overwhelming. The feel of GODs love took over and my earthly memories were once again a thing of the past and I was happy to be home in Heaven. This journey was different though. I found myself in a large hall with other souls around me and they seemed to be attempting to ease my pain and trying to make me feel warm, welcome and comfortable. But it was all without words. The hall was a large room with high ceilings that had what looked like nooks built into the walls.

The nooks had what appeared to be souls wrapped in blankets. I wasn't sure where I was and why I was there but I wasn't concerned because it felt safe. It almost felt as if I was there to be debriefed and helped through the transition back home, but no one was saying a word. It was as if they were just there to insure I was OK and to make my transition go smoothly. I felt I was cared for and I knew that it would all be OK, I just didn't know when or how. The warmth and the love I felt was even greater and more intense than my first transition in 2005. It was deeper and more caring if that is even possible. Maybe what I was experiencing this time was because my death was more traumatic.

In 2005 when I had the cardiac arrest, my body collapsed and when death came, it came quickly. When I transitioned in 2005 I was welcomed by family and loved ones and I think that was the time I was supposed to go home. But the skills of the emergency team found a way save me and bring me back to this world.

This time death was slower. Death didn't come in minutes it came over hours. This one had much more pain and suffering during this process of death. It is possible my soul wasn't ready to leave earth this time, and as I struggled to remain here my death became more distressful.

Maybe this is what happens when people die unexpectedly in a traumatic situation or are murdered or killed in an accident. Their soul wasn't ready or wasn't called back at that time and the soul was in shock. Perhaps this group of Angel's sole purpose is to insure your transition is as painless as possible. Maybe the other souls I saw in the nooks were in some sort of hibernation to ease a traumatic transition. Maybe those souls need to heal from its trauma and will eventually be blessed with GODs mercy and glory. I can only speculate why it was this way and perhaps when I do make my final journey I will understand it more.

I had more to lose than the first time and therefore I fought harder to remain on earth. I don't know if this is the proper way to decipher this but it is all I can think of for some sort of explanation.

Is there a proper way to make the journey to the afterlife? No one can answer that question. Those of us that have made that journey and are still here to speak of it or willing to speak of it are the only ones to know how their individual transition occurred.

ᴄ⁄ᴏ ᴏ⁄ᴏ

Then once again I felt the rush backwards as I was being returned to earth. There was no warning that it was going to happen, no knowledge of why I had to return, not a word was said and I was just being sent back and once again the medical team at the hospital found a way to resuscitate me.

I don't know how long it took to bring me back to life. The next thing I remember, I was on a gurney in the hall way outside of the hospital room. I remember being wheeled past my wife and some of our friends and the Hospital Chaplin who was there to give me the last rites.

The fear in their eyes and their reactions affirmed the critical condition I was in. They tried to talk to me and touch me but were moved away by the staff.

The nurses told them that we had to move and move fast as they took off in a trot down the hallway. They rushed me to another floor and into an intensive care unit to prep me for emergency surgery. This was not an easy thing to be conscious during. I begged for medication but they wouldn't give me anything for the pain or to put me to sleep while they prepped me. My vital signs were still all over the board and medications could cause death.

My savior in the surgical ICU prep room was a nurse by the name of Mary. She told me what they were going to do. They had to put a tube down my nose into my stomach to pump out the blood. I told her I did not want this and she told me point blank that if we don't do this I will die. She told me I had to swallow in order to get the tube down into the stomach.

She told me to look into her eyes and that she wasn't going to lose me today. I had my doubts, I already went once and now the pain is worse and I am hanging on to life by a thread. While they were trying to push a tube into my nose and down into my stomach another nurse was putting in a urinary catheter. As she was doing that a third nurse was putting in a groin arterial I.V. with numerous I.V. leads in order to pump in large quantities of blood at one time. All I could see was the tube running past my right eye as the blood was being pulled from my stomach. Mary kept telling me not to look at the tube, but to look into her eyes and that she had me. I looked away from her and saw four pints of blood on the I.V. holder flowing into the leads that were flowing into the artery in my groin.

I had no idea if all those in the waiting room had any idea of what happening and I am so glad at that moment they did not. This was a horrible experience to be conscience for.

I kept gagging on the tube causing me to throw up, but all that was left was blood. As the bags of blood are being pushed into my system the tube in my nose is pumping the blood from my stomach and blood was spewing out of my mouth all over me and Mary, but she never faltered, she never looked away from me, she never let go of my hand. They were able to pump out enough blood to slow the intense pain and I also stopped vomiting blood. All through this, Mary never left my side; she truly was an angel of mercy.

The blood was still being pumped in and coming out the tube because of the tear in my esophagus. They got me stable enough to give me a shot of medication to relax me in order to move me into surgery. I asked Mary to tell my wife Lisa something for me and she said you tell her yourself.

I said no, she can't see me this way, she said "we will clean you up" and I will get her. They cleaned me up, cleaned the area and the bed up and Mary (I am sure she changed her scrubs) was prepping my wife and the others in the waiting room about my condition and what my wife will see. I was attached to machines, numerous tubes and IV's were attached to me and my color was still grey because death was pulling me one way and the hospital staff was pulling me the other way to save me. Then Mary walked Lisa into the room. My heart hurt for what she had to see and endure and I was amazed at how strong she was. I am blessed in more ways than one to have her in my life. Once Lisa left the room they moved me to surgery to repair the damage to my esophagus.

⋙ ⋘

I lost the majority of my blood, my heart rate was not stable and it took two clamps to stop the bleeding in my esophagus. It took 11 pints of blood to keep me alive and get my hemoglobin back to a minimum level of 8.9 to allow my body to start to produce its own hemoglobin.

I was moved to a room on the intensive care unit after surgery. I was in critical condition; and they still were not sure I would make it through the night. I had a fever of 103. I overheard the nurses tell my wife that if I could break this fever I would have a good chance of surviving. As I lay there going in and out of consciousness some of our other close friends came in to possibly say their last goodbyes.

Corky and Lisa had called them and told them to get to the hospital and that it may be the last time they would see me alive. The following morning my fever broke and it looked like I was going to pull through. Over the next couple of days many of my friends came to ICU to visit.

This was still a critical time and you know the value of friendship in a time like this. You learn to appreciate these people and hold them close in your heart. Love is the best prescription for healing.

9

The Naughty Nursing Care

It is amazing how in less than twenty four hours things can go so badly. After what I had just been through, I couldn't believe a hospital of this caliber would employ such trash as these nurses that I encountered. I spent three days in the critical care ICU unit on the fourth floor and my care was excellent and my nursing staff was compassionate and highly qualified. On May 1st I improved enough that they decided to move me to an ICU step down unit on the third floor. The unit is the same as the fourth floor ICU. It has twenty beds, all single rooms with 1 nurse assigned to two patients. I was also told by a nurse on the floor, there are typically twelve nurses per shift, a supervisor, Nurses Assistants and a secretary.

I was moved to the third floor about 6:00 PM. The next morning my assigned nurse, Lisa Z., removed my urinary catheter and had me up and walking in the hall per doctor orders. Half way through the walk I had another syncope episode and was returned to bed. The rapid response team was called again. They stabilized me and I was placed on bed arrest. I was now restricted to bed and I know I am monitored because of the blackouts.

My wife got to the hospital about 3:00 PM. I rang the nurse's button for assistance to use the restroom for a bowel movement. It had been over four days. They answered the call almost immediately that they would be there in just a few moments. Eight to ten minutes passed and no one had arrived. (My intent was not lessening).

I started to get angry and decided to remove a few of my heart monitor leads to see if that would move them along. We hear the call over the overhead speakers with my room number that they were getting no response from the heart monitor.

Again, no one came in and after an additional three or four minutes I had to go! I removed the rest of the leads and I moved myself to the restroom. Shortly after I went into the restroom, three nurses arrived, not one of them was my nurse Lisa Z. They seemed angry when they came in. One was young with short brown hair, another, named Amber B with short blonde/brown hair in a bob and the worst one of all (I do not have her name) she had big eyes, curly brown hair and was short and stocky. She rushed into the bathroom and instead of being concerned, she arrived with a negative attitude and angrily yelled (yes, yelled) at me that I was "not complying and I shouldn't be in the bathroom alone and this is unacceptable behavior". I responded by hitting the soiled garment bag lid in front of me with my hand and yelled back that if she would have come when I called, I wouldn't have to go by myself. At that time she grabbed Nurse Amber B. walked out and yelled "we don't need to put up with this call security."

I am not a man that would instigate fear from the sheer size of my form. Remember what my condition is and I am only in a gown sitting on a toilet. The younger nurse with the short brown hair was very nice asked if she could put a mobile heart monitor on me and that immediately calmed me down and I agreed to the monitor. After all I just needed to use the bathroom. She said I will go get one and the shorter stocky one said you are out of there and she never returned with my monitor.

My wife hears all of this insanity about security and she gets involved and asked the short stocky one to please leave she will take care of me. Security arrived in the hallway outside of my room and Amber B. tells security to get her out of here (referring to removing my wife from the hospital grounds).

Now please keep in mind, I am a critical care patient, who just a few days prior had died and was resuscitated, and it took 11 pints of blood to keep me alive. I have syncope problems, and I am also a cardiac patient who is recovering from major surgery.

The only ones in the room were me and my forty seven year old, school teacher wife. Now this next bit of story is so far out there that you can't make this stuff up!

SEVEN security officers descend on my room as in a Gestapo style raid. (You can't make this kind of stuff up!) A new young, blonde haired security officer told my wife to leave and she refused. He moved toward my wife and said, "You will go if I want you to."

I got quite agitated and moved toward the young guard. An older security officer, his name was Fred (not his real name), saw I was starting to get extremely agitated and my level of decorum was gone and he removed the young guard from the room and stated he would get us a manager to discuss this situation.

Now, remember, I am still unhooked from the heart monitors and no one from the nursing staff returned to hook me up and I am in an high stress position with a police force in abundance in my ICU room. I dialed 911 for Royal Oak Police Department to help me. I agreed with R.O.P.D. to discuss this situation with Fred the senior security officer on site. Then a Nursing Manager (not from this floor) came in to discuss this with us because the actual floor manager was off campus. The Nursing Manager listened to my story, and then I told her, that my nurse, Lisa Z. wasn't there. She also listened to my wife's side of the story. She was very defensive of the staff and acted as if we were lying. This was such bad behavior from a manager in a well-known hospital facility.

It is apparent that if Lisa Z. left the floor she did not insure proper coverage of her patients, all 2 of us.

All the while we were talking to the Nursing Manager, nurse Amber B. stood in the door way smirking and being very unprofessional and acting like she was still in grade school. We asked the Manager to move me off the floor so we would not have to deal with such unprofessional care providers. The Nursing Manager then cleared security from the room and left to speak with the nurses involved.

The Lt. of Security arrived in the hall and listened to the Nursing Manager interview the nurses involved. After a few moments, the Lt. of Security and the Nursing Manager walked into my room and shut my door.

They immediately agreed to move me to a room on the fourth floor and the Managers demeanor was very different. The LT. even admitted to my wife and I that she could tell the nurses actions was inappropriate and their stories did not sound factual. The Lt. of Security also went to high school with my wife so she stayed a bit longer and chatted with us.

I was moved to the fourth floor by a Nurses Asst. and Nurses Lisa Z. and Amber B. All the way to the new floor they smiled, smirked and acted like grade school girls. Once in my new room Amber B. removed my transport heart monitor and grabbed the new leads for the monitor in the room and instead of putting them on me, dropped them in my lap and said to the new RN "I gotta get out of here, it's too hot" and left the room.

I also came to find out Lisa Z. worked on the fourth floor. Now I was concerned about the information the staff on this floor may have received and I did not feel comfortable or safe. This was a very trying day so far.

I wrote the President of the Hospital a letter that evening via e-mail and also addressed it to the CEO, the head of the board of directors and the head of Cardiac Nursing. The hospital President responded quickly that evening and sent in a Nurse Administrator to speak with me.

She arrived at approximately 9 PM. We discussed the details of this incident in detail and she did say the actions of the nurses were "incorrigible." She also mentioned she taught nursing for eighteen years and that nurses are taught to act in a completely different manor.

The following morning, at 9 AM, the Hospital President, the head of Cardiac Nursing and a leadership trainee came to my room.

They asked me what I thought should happen to the staff in question. I stated that I felt that Amber B. and the short stocky nurse needed to be terminated and empting bed-pans at Wayne County Jail by that afternoon. I think they were quite shocked by my statement.

I did tell those present that I was not going to let this go as the nurse's behavior was extremely inappropriate. I then had two immediate demands. The first was to move me back to the 8th floor South Tower in a private room, where I was originally because it is where I felt safe and had a tremendous relationship with the staff.

The 2nd was to have the Nurses involved apologize to my wife and me in front of a senior staff member for their actions. Per my request I was moved to the 8th floor that day and nothing else regarding the hospitals investigation, or the reprimands was mentioned to me again nor did an apology ever happen.

I did file a complaint against the Hospital and the four nurses with the State Board of Health. After a couple of months, the State of Michigan responded and stated they did not have sufficient evidence to proceed since I was not given the names of the nurses involved. The President of the hospital refused to release the full name of the nurses involved because they felt that I may try to cause them physical harm. How absolutely ridiculous!

When they moved me back to the eighth floor the head of Cardiac Nursing was there to greet me and insure I was comfortable in my new room.

Several of the nurses and nursing assistants I knew prior came in immediately to welcome me back. I could see the Head of Nursing was shocked at the rapport I had with this staff. She left shortly after that only to be seen once again.

I wish to state that throughout my seventeen day ordeal in this Hospital in Royal Oak, MI. that all the staff and especially the staff on floor eight south were tremendous. This incident has not deterred me from this hospital. But now I know what and where I need to be if I ever have to return.

Maybe the nurses in question were having a bad day. Maybe they were not happy that they had to help more than 2 patients since my nurse was off the floor. Whatever the reason their behavior was totally unacceptable and I am shocked that they still may have a job.

A few months later my wife ran into her friend from the hospital. She told my wife that the hospital instituted an education program that they originally put on hold because of the costs to teach it. The course is about patient care, patient treatment and patient respect by the staff and that she was one of the instructors. All hospital employees are required to take this course because of this incident. So I do suppose something good did come out of this event.

The lesson to be learned by this event; Do not hesitate to contact the senior management of the hospital. Your care or the care of your loved one is the priority and you should insure that you are receiving the best possible care you can get. Hospitals do not want bad press!

10

The Diagnosis

After I was out of ICU and back on the eighth floor, my cardiologist came in and diagnosed my syncope episodes as a disorder called Dysautonomia which is a chronicle disorder which affects the autonomic nervous system. That was very disturbing news as my life was now changing yet again. I was told I couldn't drive for 6 months; walking without passing out was now a daily goal. I often have to stop to rest. I had to change my way of thinking and what I used to do in a day; can now take me several days or more to complete. Exertion causes shortness of breath and moving too quickly can cause lightheadedness. Anxiety is at its peak and has not alleviated to this day. Every day with this disorder is an adventure. Some days I feel better and other days I curse having to deal with this. I knew I needed additional help in the determination and potential solutions or ways to cope with this disorder.

On May 7th I was discharged from the hospital after seventeen days of pain, suffering and disappointment. We made arrangements to see a specialist and it took over a month and a half to secure an appointment at the Cleveland Clinic.

We went to see a Dysautonomia specialist at the Cleveland Clinic on July 2nd with additional testing scheduled on July 3rd. We spent the night in Cleveland and went through the battery of tests that were scheduled. After all the tests were completed we returned to Michigan and my doctors here placed me on a mix of medications and I have had no major syncope episodes. I still get the lightheadedness, shortness of breath, dizzy, fatigue, but no full syncope episodes.

The specialist also diagnosed me with Small Fiber Neuropathy and suggested I see another specialist, Dr. Yi, at the Cleveland Clinic Neurological Center. I saw this specialist on the 20th of September 2012.

Dr. Yi went through my medical records from my stay in the hospital page by page. He spent over two hours with us and he saw the pattern in the symptoms versus the hemoglobin ranges on the lab reports. The lab reports clearly show I was bleeding internally with the drop in hemoglobin and thus the cause for the full syncope was anemia. My hemoglobin dropped over three points over a four day span. Finally some explanations to the madness, the trip to Cleveland has paid off yet again.

Dr. Yi also believes that the small fiber neuropathy and the dysautonomia were caused by my death and subsequent resuscitation when my body was "reset". He feels that when I was resuscitated that my nervous system didn't respond correctly and thus caused my current symptoms.

My Gastroenterologist, who repaired the damage on my esophagus, did an EDG at the end of July to see the how the damage was healing. He found ulcers in my stomach and one of the clips used to close the hole in my esophagus did not fall off as it should have, and he had to remove it. The site started to bleed again and he had to inject the spot with a drug to seal the hole and stop the bleeding. The tissue in that area is now dead because of the drug used to seal the hole and has the potential to break open in the future. He scheduled another EDG for September 7th as a follow up to see how we are healing. In that procedure he found numerous ulcers. I tested negative for the Pylori bacteria which is the primary cause of ulcers on four different occasions. We do not know the reason for these ulcers and current testing is ongoing. He believes I had bleeding ulcers at the damaged spot in my esophagus and that caused the drop in my hemoglobin while in the hospital and when I vomited from the blood filling my stomach it tore the damaged spot wide open.

The correlation of events determined by the Neurologist at the Cleveland Clinic seems to be in line with this diagnosis. I was blessed to be in the hospital at the time of this bleed out. It is agreed that I would not have survived the damage and blood loss that I had if I did not have immediate care in the hospital.

The trauma of my death and resuscitation, the damage and stress to my body could have been avoided if the drop in Hemoglobin was brought to the attention of the doctors on the 27th of April prior to the surgery for the Loop Recorder Implant. No one saw it or didn't feel it that a three point drop in hemoglobin was substantial enough to report it.

I began to see my Therapist again because my mental health has been compromised due to this event. I am dealing with a form of Post-Traumatic Stress Disorder due to dying on the 29th of April and now it has escalated with the knowledge that it all could have been avoided with one person raising a red flag at the drop in hemoglobin prior to a surgery.

Can you imagine listening to the nurse countdown your heartbeats left in your life? Can you imagine knowing that you are on your way out and your life is over? Can you imagine looking into the eyes of your spouse and still have the mental capacity to know this is the last time you will ever see her/him again? Traumatic? Stressful? That doesn't even scratch the surface of how this feels to have to deal with on a daily basis.

The Stress of the Insurance Battles

I have been unable to work since April 21st. Once my short term disability expired in mid-July, Cigna Insurance denied my long term disability. (I also have been paying an additional insurance premium for long term disability coverage through my employer.)

This is so very disturbing when a person is trying to recuperate and heal. My full time job now became dealing with insurance companies. There were the phone calls and the emails and the collection of documents from my Doctors for the insurance company. There was the letter of appeal and the subsequent conference calls.

Then they switch your contact at the company that you have built some sort of rapport with over the past few months and now you have someone completely new to deal with. It is a never ending frustrating process. I did not have income from July through September and I used my saving to stay afloat. All of this has also caused an enormous amount of stress, and additional depression that I did not need during this difficult time. As of the end of September 2012, I was finally notified that my long term disability denial had finally been overturned and I would begin to receive income again until we can come to a conclusion on my medical challenges.

Insurance companies need serious reform. People that are hurt, both mentally and physically do not need the additional stress that insurance companies put on you. Your physicians can insert a couple of different words in their report and you are suddenly denied; aggravation becomes an understatement. We are trying to recover on both levels and then to have the additional stress of insurance rejections is an abomination to the poor souls who want nothing more than to try to return to normalcy and continue on with their lives. I suggest we all write our political leaders and push for pressure to be put on Insurance companies. Premiums are paid to have the safety net and when that net is needed there shouldn't be a fight to get what we paid our hard earned money for.

The best thing you can do is to be vigilant, educate yourself on your particular disorder and keep an open line of communication with your insurance company representatives and stay on top of your Physicians' offices.

Make sure they get their reports out in a timely fashion to the insurance company and insure you have copies of all of the reports. Yes, it is a lot of work for someone that needs to be resting and healing, but our insurance system has so many flaws we must do it ourselves in order to protect ourselves.

Educating yourself on your health disorder is critical. If you do not understand what and why you are ill, how can you understand the reasoning behind the decisions of the insurance companies or even the Doctors? You know what and how you feel but it is advantageous to understand the reason why. This way you can argue the points that the insurance companies will try to use to deny your claims.

The other suggestion is find someone or a group that you can talk to that knows and understands your particular challenge. Often you will feel that you are all alone in your challenges even though you have a spouse and family surrounding you. It isn't their fault. They are trying to be supportive but after they hear of your pains and problems for so long it begins to fall on deaf ears. You must remember they do not have what you have. They do not feel what you are feeling. Others out there know these things and to find that person or persons will be a blessing. I personally found someone through a friend who has the disorder I have and she has been dealing with this for years. Talking to her made me feel that I wasn't alone and it gave me hope that I can get through this. Yes, her life is changed from what it once was. She was a full time teacher, and now she can only teach a couple of days a week and she is a substitute now. But, she is still alive and able to function most days. What she would do in a day now takes a few to complete and I know how that feels. She will have bad days and she will have good days as I do. But she says over time it does get somewhat better.

There is a light at the end of the tunnel and this tunnel is an adjustment to the way you do things in your life. It is a learned process that takes time. I will get through this and you will too.

Social Security Disability

Part of the long term disability process is, I had to apply for social security disability. This, friendly readers, is the biggest sham and if you thought insurance companies were difficult to deal with then you are in for a horrible surprise with SSDI. If there is a government program that needs to be changed from the ground up, it is SSDI. Over 75% of all first time Social Security Disability applications are denied.

The social security representatives are cold and unproductive. I think they just go through the paces knowing in advance you will be turned down. They put forth a minimal effort to secure medical documentation. I tried to send in what I could get from my doctors. She also knew I was seeing a psychologist about the Post Traumatic Stress Disorder and she refused to accept a report from my Doctor. She sent me to their social security psychologist which was nothing but a pure joke.

The office was in the 'hood' and was old and dirty and disgusting. She was not of American decent and I would like to see her true credentials. The office was 1 room and a waiting room with some machine playing earth sounds so loud to cover up the conversation in the other room. Her office was a mess, disorganized and musty. You could hardly understand a word she said and in a 50 minute interview she determined I was fine. What a crock and a waste of tax payer dollars. I have been seeing my psychologist for 7 months and we are still working through the challenges and this "doctor" can make a call in less than an hour? This system needs to be revamped!

I also had informed the Social Security representative that I had an 11 hour neuro-psych exam coming up and she ignored the test and refused to wait for the results. Once I completed the eleven hours of neuropsychological exams the results show that I have severe depression and post-traumatic stress disorder.

The doctor states that the depression and anxiety make it difficult for me to work at this time; The Doctors recommendation is I could possibly return to work in a year after a re-evaluation. This was critical information to my determination by Social Security and they wouldn't wait a few days for the results.

Cigna's long term policy does supply a company that is free of charge to assist in securing Social Security. This was another waste of time. The company is called Advantage 2000 and the initial team are not paralegals or attorneys but people who say they are trying to get you your SSDI but actual do nothing. Since I have been denied by Social Security it was turned over to the Advantage 2000 legal team and an attorney is involved as of February of 2013, when I originally applied for SSDI in July of 2012. Now this process begins all over again. I am told to get in front of an administrative judge will take six months to a year. So, do you see what is happening here America? The Insurance company employs a group of people which is a waste of money under the guise that they are trying to help with the advance knowledge that over 75% are turned down the first time around and then after months of 'nothing' they refer you to their legal team. Now would it not be wiser to disband this group of people, hire a few more paralegals and attorneys' and turn all the cases over to legal immediately? More waste of your insurance premiums.

Dealing with Insurance companies and social security disability is truly a traumatic event all in itself. You find yourself praying to GOD a lot during these struggles. You dig deep into your spirituality having to deal with so many uncaring people. It makes recovery so difficult and the only one that seems to care is you.

It is quite the scam; let's look at the web of Insurance Companies and Social Security Disability. My short term disability ran out in 3 months (July 2012). Cigna then denied my long term disability and through the appeal process it took until September 2012 to be approved. During which time, I utilized my savings to pay the bills. I applied for SSDI in July 2012 (when short term expired), I was denied within 3 months and SSDI would not wait for two reports from two PHD Psychologists which are critical to my case. It is now February 2013 and I finally was able to get SSDI to take the reports and add it to my file after an hour wait at the local SS office. I also now have legal representation when I should have had it in October of 2012. So we lost five months of critical time and the hope is that I will buckle and stop the SSDI process and return to work whether I am able to or not.

An appeal hearing was just granted. But, the hearing date won't be for 6 to 12 months. In April 2013, my long term ends. The soonest I will get a hearing is July 2013. Now I anticipate I will be approved because the two reports specifically state that I should not be working for a minimum of one year pending a re-evaluation of my condition. This would leave me without income or health insurance coverage for a minimum of 3 months to a maximum of 9 months or more. How do they expect people to survive? The answer; the government does not care about us.

Now let me ask you, the reader, what is wrong with this picture? A person pays into social security all his working life. In my case 36 years. Now I do believe I will be able to return to work but it may take me another year, possibly less. So why does our government deny us the money we have placed in their care (without interest) and allow us the time we need to recover? Why is it wrong for a person in my situation to collect SSDI for a year until I am capable of returning to work? Why the government can't set a guideline that a company must accept a person back within a 1 year timeframe is unknown. The government wants to get involved in business does it not?

After all, it is my money that I have already paid into the system that I would be getting back. We threw billions of dollars at GM and Chrysler, and lending institutions that the government claims "are too big to fail", but they can't rebuild the Social Security Administration.

Our system is broken and it will take action to repair it and not leave it in the hands of the idiots who are currently running our country into the ground. As Americans it is not only our right but our obligation to tell our elected officials that our system is broke and they need to repair it. If they can't fix it, then do not re-elect them and let's get somebody in there who will try and if they won't then they get fired too. This is not a political soap box of one party vs. the other. They both have their good policies and they both have their bad ones. But the onus is on us to protect ourselves from the tyranny of government.

The insurance companies are very intertwined with the government. The insurance companies have their lawyers. The laws that are affecting all of us are written by politicians who are also lawyers and the government then has their lawyers look it over. The laws are not written to benefit the American people. Laws are written to benefit the government. Unfortunately too many Americans look to the government for guidance and assistance. Americans have to get that 1945 spirit back into their hearts and not be afraid to fight and work and produce to make this the greatest country on earth once again. It is time for Americans to take responsibility for themselves.

As it is now the hamster wheel starts turning, government stalls, nothing good gets accomplished and our Constitution begins to be used as wallpaper.

So what can you do to help yourself? I am glad you asked that question.

Keep your faith and spirituality; you will need it to get through this. Be vigilant and be your own advocate. Stay on the insurance companies and never be afraid to ask for a supervisor. Do not take their answer as fact. The person you may be speaking with has minimal power and discretionary powers at best. Keep pushing the envelope and never settle. It is your life and your medical challenges and they have no idea how you feel or how it is affecting you. Although it is difficult, tiring and exhausting, it needs to be done to protect you and it does have a benefit. It keeps you alive at the same time; it gives you a meaning and a purpose when your situation may be dark and clouded.

There is a fight or flight instinct in our bodies. By sitting back and taking the flight instinct and hoping the insurance company will be good to you and Social Security will actually have an ounce of compassion or empathy for you, then you become the victim.

This is a time to use your fight instinct. Stand up for yourself. You are the one that holds you closer to your heart than anyone else. So use what GOD has installed in you and fight for your rights.

11

Religious Views of the Afterlife

❦

Knowing what my experiences were only made me wonder what other religions believe about the afterlife. So I did a bit of research and here are some examples of what various faiths believe concerning the afterlife. I thought this may be interesting to evaluate and also to see the relationship between the different faiths and religions.

Bahá'í Faith

Bahá'í beliefs are sometimes described as different combinations of earlier religious beliefs. The Bahá'ís faith, state that their religion is distinctly individual with its own teachings, scripture, rules, and history. The religion was initially seen as a sect of Islam, but most religious specialists now see it as an independent religion.

The teachings of the Bahá'í Faith state that the soul is immortal and after death it will continue to progress until it attains God's presence. In Bahá'í belief, souls in the afterlife will continue to retain their individuality and consciousness and will be able to recognize and communicate spiritually with other souls whom they have made deep profound friendships with, such as their spouses.

Prior to my research, I have held this belief. I find it invigorating to find such teachings and to learn about the concepts of other religions than my own. This is a logical belief to me based on my own death experiences. I seem to learn something new every day; learning isn't just for the young folks.

Islamic Faith

The Islamic belief in the afterlife as stated in the Qur'an is very descriptive. The Islamic word for Paradise is Jannat and Hell is Jahannam.

Jannat and Jahannam both have different levels. Jannat has eight gates and eight levels. The higher the level the better it is and the happier you are. Jahannam possess seven deep terrible layers. The lower the layer the worse it is. Their level of comfort while in the grave depends wholly on their level of faith in Allah.

The Arabic word "Islam" means the submission or surrender of one's will to the only true god worthy of worship "Allah" and anyone who does so is termed a "Muslim", The word also implies "peace" which is the natural consequence of total submission to the will of Allah. It is a true religion brought by Prophet Muhammad in Arabia dating back to the seventh century.

The Detroit area is where the largest United States population of the Muslim religion resides. As such, I have known and do know many people that practice the Muslim faith. These people aren't any different than you and I. They want better lives for themselves and their families as non-Muslims want. They work hard and enjoy the same freedoms non-Muslims do. They are Americans.

The events of September 11, 2001 and September 11, 2012 do not fairly depict the people, the Americans, which practice this religion. In all religions we will find a radical sect that will try to place their insane beliefs onto others.

We can only pray that these radicals will be put down by the true people of their faiths and beliefs of the individual religions.

I pray that all people will see that as individuals we have our own religious beliefs and we worship our own supreme being whether his name is GOD, Allah, Buddha or Brahman. Doing so, we will be able to have an understanding of each other and find peace with each other.

I have many Muslim friends and I have spoken with them concerning what their beliefs are in the Muslim faith. If you do not learn how can you criticize? The Qur'an is their Holy Book. Just as the Bible is the Holy Book for Christians. Most Muslims regard the Qur'an with extreme honor; they will wrap it in a clean cloth, keeping it on a high shelf. Old Qur'ans are not destroyed as wastepaper, but deposited in Qur'an graveyards. The Qur'an is regarded as a true guide to personal devotion and life.

There are no Muslim images or depictions of God because such artistic depictions may lead to a form of a cult following and are prohibited. Many Muslims believe that God is lacking any type of material form, making any visual images impossible.

At the time of death in the Muslim faith the Imam will come and wash the body of the deceased and then wrap it in an unbleached cloth prior to being turned over to a funeral home for viewing and burial.

The Muslim creed in English: "I believe in God; and in His Angels; and in His Scriptures; and in His Messengers; and in The Final Day; and in Fate that Good and Evil are from God, and Resurrection after death is Truth."

Notable messengers include Adam, Noah, Abraham, Moses, Jesus, and Muhammad, all belonging to a succession of men guided by God. Mainstream Muslims regard Muhammad as the 'Last Messenger'.

The Catholic Faith

The Catholic conception of the afterlife teaches after the body dies, the soul is judged, the righteous and free of sin enter Heaven. However, those who die in un-repented mortal sin go to hell. In the 1990s, the Catechism of the Catholic Church defined hell not as punishment imposed on the sinner but rather as the sinner's self-exclusion from God.

Unlike other Christian groups, the Catholic Church teaches that those who die in a state of grace, but still carry sin will go to a place called Purgatory where they undergo purification to enter Heaven. I have not found this to be true in my experiences. In my opinion Purgatory is here on earth and how we act here will determine our final stop. In my case, I feel I need to atone for sins and thus I was sent back to earth to find peace within myself. Once again it is all speculation but I can't find any other explanations.

Jewish Faith

Jewish sacred texts and literature have little to say about what happens after death. This may seem surprising to non-Jews, since the sacred texts of Christianity and Islam (both of which have their foundations in Judaism) elaborate rather fully about the afterlife. The Torah and Talmud alike focus on the purpose of earthly life, which is to fulfill one's duties to God and one's fellow man. Succeeding at this brings reward, failing at it brings punishment.

Whether rewards and punishments continue after death, or whether anything at all happens after death, is not as important. Life after death is not denied nor confirmed.

Mormon Faith

Joseph F. Smith of The Church of Jesus Christ of Latter-day Saints presents an elaborate vision of the Afterlife. It is revealed as the scene of an extensive missionary effort by righteous spirits to redeem those still in darkness — a spirit prison or "hell" where the spirits of the dead remain until judgment. It is divided into two parts: Spirit Prison and Paradise. Together these are also known as the Spirit World where they will undergo instruction and preparation. Then, "after a time," there will be the Resurrection, at which time the spirits will be reunited with their bodies forever.

Mormons believe in heaven, which is defined as "the place where God lives and the future home of those who follow Him." Faithful

Mormons and their families will live in the presence of God and be rewarded in accordance with what they have done during their lives.

Buddhist Faith

Buddha was an Indian mystic and the founder of Buddhism. He went from a life of luxury and gave that up to attain supreme enlightenment. He began preaching after achieving supreme enlightenment when he was in his thirties. Buddhism's basic doctrines include reincarnation and karma, as well as the notion that the ultimate goal of the religious life is to escape the cycle of death and rebirth by reaching Nirvana which is the Buddhist term for liberation. Nirvana literally means extinction, and it refers to the extinction of all earthly cravings.

Buddha differed from the Hinduism faith in "anatta", which is the concept that individuals do not have eternal souls.

Instead of eternal souls, individuals consist of a various desires, sensations, habits, memories, when combined makes one think that they now consist of a lasting self.

Per Tibetan Buddhism, following death the deceased's spirit goes through a process lasting forty-nine days that is divided into three stages called bardos. At the conclusion of the bardo, the person either enters nirvana or returns to earth for rebirth. It is extremely important that the dying individual remain fully conscience for as long as possible because the thoughts that they have while passing over into death will influence the nature of both the after-death experience and, if they do not achieve nirvana, it will influence the state of their next incarnation.

Buddhists maintain that rebirth takes place without an unchanging self or soul passing from one form to another. The type of rebirth will be conditioned by the person's actions or karma. For example, where a person has committed harmful actions of body, speech and mind based on greed, hatred and delusion, rebirth in a lower realm, such as an animal, a ghost or a hell realm, is to be expected. On the other hand, where a person has performed skillful actions based on generosity, loving-kindness, compassion and wisdom, rebirth in a happy realm, i.e. human or one of the many heavenly realms can be expected.

Sikh Faith

The Sikh religion was founded by Guru Nanak. It is stated in the Sikh texts that Guru Nanak while in deep meditation by a river was called to the court of God where he received direct revelations from God for three days. It is stated that God asked Nanak to drink from the cup of Naam which is the Essence of God and then promoted Nanak to the highest of all status.

From there on God sent him forward as Guru Nanak so that he could teach the world that there is one God, that all humanity is one, and that religious divisions are man-made.

Sikhs also believe in reincarnation. They believe that the soul belongs to the spiritual universe which has its origins in God. It is like a see-saw, the amount of good done in life will store up blessings, thus uniting with God. It needs to be clarified whether the ideal is union or link with 'Waheguru' (God) or merger in God.

Hinduism

Hinduism is the prominent religion of the continent of India. Hinduism includes Shaivism, Vaishnavism and Śrauta as well as many other traditions. Hinduism is a very complex faith and is not only one of the largest faiths, but is also the oldest living tradition on earth, dating back into prehistory. Hinduism was also formed by many different traditions and there is no single founder of this form of religion. Hinduism also holds the belief of reincarnation that is determined by the laws of karma. Buddhism, Jainism and Sikhism, also believe in the law of karma. It is also the world's third largest religion only behind Christianity and Islam.

Hinduism recognizes numerous divine beings that are subordinate to the Supreme Being. Hinduism is complete freedom of belief and worship. The Hinduism belief is the whole world is a single family that holds the one truth, and it accepts all forms of beliefs and dismisses labels of other standard religions which would show a difference in identity. A person that practices the Hindu belief believes that the concept of God is complex and varies based on each individual and their particular tradition and philosophy that they follow.

Most Hindus believe that the spirit or soul is the true "self" of every person, and that soul (called the atman) is eternal. Upon death in the Hindu faith as well as the Sikh faith the families will wash the bodies of the deceased themselves. Males will tend to the bodies of males and females will care for the female deceased.

In death, cremation is considered the proper form to set the 'atman' free for all except for sanyasis (It is considered the topmost and final stage of the ashram systems and is traditionally taken by men or women over fifty or by young monks who wish to renounce worldly and materialistic pursuits and dedicate their lives to spiritual pursuits), hijra (In southern Asia, hijras are physiological males who have feminine gender identity, adopt feminine gender roles, and wear women's clothing) and children under five. Cremation is typically performed by wrapping the body in cloth and burning it on a pyre.

All of the above do have some form of the afterlife. Some reflect a heaven and hell and some reflect a reincarnation of the soul. There are many similarities in the beliefs we see above.

For some reason we hold such different religious stances against each other. I have only touched on the better known religions and there are many more. I find it amazing that of the religions above they all have their personal visions of what happens to the soul after death. These religions are all very old and although each is different they all reflect the world of the hereafter. If these ancient religions are somewhat on the same page then why in today's society does the scientific world deny the near death or death experience that those of us who have crossed the threshold have experienced?

12

Science and Near Death Experiences

This work wouldn't be complete without investigating the scientist's beliefs in the "near death experience". So in this chapter we will look at the scientific viewpoints. I will not say scientific evidence because I do not believe there is any evidence that can be presented to dispute what people like me have experienced. Some people (the scientific community) believe in the old adage; "I will believe it when I see it." In the company I work for we have sayings that we call ISM's. One ISM we use is; "When you see it, you will believe it". In this instance I think this may be a much better approach.

We will look at various scientific notions based on how the brain supposedly works at the moment of death, but unfortunately in this study, no one was able to be resuscitated to provide evidence of these works.

Another study used LSD to try and duplicate the Near Death Experience. I must admit I cannot see the value of this study when illegal narcotics are used to try to make a scientific statement.

First of all we need the actual definition of a Near Death Experience. Per the Wikipedia definition, "A near-death experience (NDE) refers to a broad range of personal experiences associated with impending death, encompassing multiple possible sensations including detachment from the body; feelings of levitation; total serenity, security, or warmth; the experience of absolute dissolution; and the presence of a light.

These phenomena are usually reported after an individual has been pronounced clinically dead or otherwise very close to death, hence the term near-death experience.

Many NDE reports, however, originate from events that are not life-threatening. With recent developments in cardiac resuscitation, the number of reported NDEs has increased.

The experiences have been described in medical journals as having the characteristics of hallucinations, while parapsychologists, religious believers and some mainstream scientists have pointed to them as evidence of an afterlife and mind-body dualism."

Near death experiences can be traced back to the works of Plato in the 4th century BC. This is the oldest surviving report of a NDE in Western literature. It is the story of Er who was a soldier who awoke on his funeral pyre and described his journey into the afterlife. Plato integrated at least three elements of the NDE into his philosophy. Those three elements are the departure of the soul to see the light, the flight of the soul to a vision of pure celestial being and its recollection of the vision of light, which is the very purpose of philosophy.

Here are the words that Plato wrote:

"..The tale of a warrior bold, Er, the son of Armenious, by race a Pamphylian. He once upon a time was slain in battle, and when the corpses were taken up on the tenth day already decayed, he was found intact, and having been brought home, at the moment of his funeral, on the twelfth day as he lay upon the pyre, revived, and after coming to life related what, he said, he had seen in the world beyond. He said that when his soul went forth from his body he journeyed with a great company and that they came to a mysterious region where there were two openings side by side in the Earth, and above and over against them in the heaven two others, and that judges were sitting between these, and that after every judgment they bade the righteous journey to the right and upward through the heaven with tokens attached to them in front of the judgment passed upon them, and the unjust to take the road to the left and downward, they too wearing behind signs of all that had befallen them, and that when he himself drew near they told him that he must be the messenger to humanity to tell them of that other world, and they charged him to give ear and to observe everything in the place."

The scientific community holds fast that the NDE is caused by certain hormones or electrical pulses being released by the brain when death is near or is occurring. I have nothing but the utmost respect for the scientific community and I know that research is dramatically needed to cure the curses of some disease in our culture. But we must also realize that science does not know all and NDEs are something that is difficult if not impossible to refute.

It certainly opens the eyes of the believers and shades the eyes of the scientists. The world cannot be seen as a place where there is an explanation and scientific explanation for all actions. There are things that we cannot explain and we must not fight it but accept that there may be more beyond this world that we live in.

Electrical Activity

One report by Dr. Lakhmir Chawla of George Washington University in Washington DC in 2009 stated that near-death experiences are caused by a "surge of electrical activity as the brain runs out of oxygen before death. Levels were similar to those seen in fully conscious people, even though blood pressure was so low as to be undetectable, and could generate vivid images and feelings."

In an interview with Skeptiko.com in 2011, Dr. Chawla also stated that all of the patients in the study passed away so there was really no way for them to know if what these people were experiencing is in fact had they survived, being the signature of a near-death experience. So in this study by Dr. Chawla we do not have a positive confirmation of his thesis.

Sensory Autonomic System Theory

In a theory by Richard Kinseher in 2006, there is the belief that the Sensory Autonomic System holds a function in a NDE. His theory states that the experience of oncoming death is contradictory to the brain or other parts of the autonomic system.

He believes that during the NDE, "the individual becomes capable of "seeing" the brain performing a scan of the whole memory, in order to find a stored experience comparable to the information of death." The theory also states that "out-of-body experiences are an attempt by the brain to create a mental estimation of the situation and the surrounding world. The brain then transforms the input from sensory organs and stored knowledge into a dream-like idea about oneself and the surrounding area. This, in turn, depends on a subconscious function of the sensory organs, rather than a total sensory loss."

The sensory side of the autonomic system is made of "sensory neurons" found in the peripheral nervous system. What these sensory neurons monitor are the levels of carbon dioxide, oxygen and sugar in the blood, arterial pressure and the chemical composition of the stomach and gut content. They also are responsible for the sense of taste and smell.

I find this theory particularly interesting since I currently have a disorder of the Autonomic Nervous System.

The Autonomic Nervous System affects heart rate, digestion, respiratory rate, salivation, perspiration, pupillary dilation, urination, and sexual arousal. This is part of Dysautonomia and in my particular case the heart rate can tachycardia (increased heart rate) or brachycardia (slowing heart rate) and it also affects my breathing as in having quicker shortness of breath. In combination I can see how they may feel that this is a viable aspect to conclude that NDEs are no more than a neurological or nervous system reaction. But after having two NDEs and also having Dysautonomia, I cannot concur with this theory.

In April of 2012, prior to my second NDE, I had approximately seven syncope episodes where there was a loss of oxygen and an increase in carbon dioxide. So I essentially acted as my own test subject unbeknownst to me and I can say I did not have any reactions that I had when I had the actual Near Death Experience.

Hallucination Theory

Some scientists believe that NDEs are going to be explained by brain functions one day. The dying brain secretes endorphins, hormones which act on the central nervous system to suppress pain. But endorphins are not hallucinogens and cannot lend itself to the experience of NDEs, so although they may be involved in the process as a form of painkiller, they are not responsible for the entire experience.

Research on neurotransmitter receptors in the brain is a very complex study and many in the field consider this type of research as in its infancy. It is medically acknowledged that a powerful anesthetic called ketamine can produce many of the features of a NDE, particularly the out-of-body element, and there is a theory that a ketamine-like substance in the brain may be released by the body at the time of a NDE. There is no scientific evidence that a substance such as ketamine is actually in the human body.

A UCLA psychology professor named Dr. Ronald Siegel rejects the spiritual and mystical concept of NDEs. He claims to have reproduced NDEs in his laboratory by giving LSD to volunteers, but, other researchers say that although drug-induced hallucinations may have some resemblance to NDEs, they are not the same. Drug induced hallucinations distort reality while NDEs have been described as "hyper-reality." So once again we do not have a firm confirmation on the non-existence of NDEs.

Dying Brain Theory

This theory is one that Dr. Susan Blackmore has taken ahold of. All those who had and reported a NDE seem to report a path toward the light, and they also report going through similar stages. This evaluation tends to make a powerful case for the whole thing being a spiritual journey to the other side. On the other side of this synopsis is the argument is that Near Death Experiences are not real experiences.

It is claimed that the NDE is a function of the brain as it is dying. All brains die in the same way, say the non-believers. As a result Dr. Blackmore and others take the stance that the neurotransmitters in the brain are shutting down and creating the same vision for all those individuals that are at or near-death.

Although this may be a possible explanation, it still cannot explain the two different experiences upon my arrival to the other-side. Each arrival was different from the other.

A Scientist Refutes His Prior Beliefs

A Neurosurgeon has had a change of his belief between science and the experience of death. He wrote a book called Proof of Heaven. He is a Neurosurgeon who happened to have had a NDE while in a coma from a meningitis infection in 2008 originally believed it was clear in that realm that the brain gives you consciousness and everything else and when the brain dies there goes consciousness and all other functions of the brain.

While he was in his coma he states that the neocortex, which is the part of the brain that is the higher brain functions such as sensory perception, was inactivated.

He said, "While the neurons of my cortex were stunned to complete inactivity by the bacteria that had attacked them, my brain-free consciousness journeyed to another, larger dimension of the universe."

I haven't personally read his book but I have read his article in Newsweek magazine. It was a very interesting cross between science and the Near Death Experience.

13

Stars and Their
Near Death Experiences

What would a Near Death Experience be without some of our greatest dramatic, comedic and musical peoples own personal experiences? So I researched and found some of their experiences in their own words. I thought this would be a nice addition to this story.

Elizabeth Taylor

Elizabeth Taylor was an icon in Hollywood. Her film credits are numerous but some of her more famous roles were National velvet, Who's Afraid of Virginia Wolf (Academy Award winner), Butterfield 8 (Academy Award winner), Cat on a Hot Tin Roof, Cleopatra and many others.

"I was pronounced dead once and actually saw the light. I find it very hard to talk about, actually, because it sounds so corny. It happened in the late '50s, and I saw Mike (Todd, Taylor's third husband, who was killed in a plane crash in 1958). When I came to, there were about 11 people in the room. I'd been gone for about five minutes - they had given me up for dead and put my death notice on the wall. I shared this with the people that were in the room next to me. Then after that I told another group of friends, and I thought, "Wow, this sounds really screwy. I think I'd better keep quiet about this."

Larry Hagman

Larry Hagman starred in "I dream of Jeanie" and also the star of the hit series Dallas. Larry Hagman underwent a liver transplant in 1995. He was only weeks away from death at the time of his liver transplant and near-death experience.

"I was able to look over the edge. I got a little glimpse of what was the next step. I didn't see a light some people see, but I had a wonderful feeling of bliss and warmth. The bottom line is love, that sounds corny, but it was just lovely, uplifting."

Sharon Stone

Stone, of the movies Basic Instinct and Casino fame says she almost died after internal bleeding caused by a tear in an artery at the base of her skull.

"When it hit me I felt like I'd been shot in the head. That's the only way I can really describe it. It hit me so hard it knocked me over on the sofa. And Phil was out of town and I called him and said, "I think I had a stroke." But in all fairness, I'm a person who's always saying, "I think I've had a stroke, I think I've had a heart attack, I think I've had a brain hemorrhage ... I had a real journey with this that took me to places both here and beyond that affected me so profoundly that my life will never be the same ... I get to be not afraid of dying and I get to tell other people that it's a fabulous thing and that death is a gift. And not that you should kill yourself, but that when death comes to you, as it will, that it's a glorious and beautiful thing. This kind of giant vortex of white light was upon me and I kind of - poof! Sort of took off into this glorious, bright, bright, bright white light and I started to see and be met by some of my friends. But it was very fast - whoosh! Suddenly, I was back. I was in my body and I was in the room."

Jane Seymore

When Jane Seymour was 36 years of old, she suffered an allergic reaction from a dose of penicillin. This led to a near-death experience.

"I literally left my body. I had this feeling that I could see myself on the bed, with people grouped around me. I remember them all trying to resuscitate me.

I was above them, in the corner of the room looking down. I saw people putting needles in me, trying to hold me down, and doing things. I remember my whole life flashing before my eyes, but I wasn't thinking about winning Emmys or anything like that. The only thing I cared about was that I wanted to live because I did not want anyone else looking after my children. I was floating up there thinking, "No, I don't want to die. I'm not ready to leave my kids." And that was when I said to God, "If you're there, God, if you really exist and I survive, I will never take your name in vain again." Although I believe that I "died" for about thirty seconds, I can remember pleading with the doctor to bring me back. I was determined I wasn't going to die."

Then she claims she suddenly found herself back in her body.

Peter Sellers

Mr. Sellers was undoubtedly known for his role as the famed Chief Inspector Clouseau in The Pink Panther films. It was in 1964, during the first of eight heart attacks, his heart stopped and he was clinically dead.

"Well, I felt myself leave my body. I just floated out of my physical form and I saw them cart my body away to the hospital. I went with it ... I wasn't frightened or anything like that because I was fine; and it was my body that was in trouble.

I looked around myself and I saw an incredibly beautiful bright loving white light above me. I wanted to go to that white light more than anything. I've never wanted anything more. I know there was love, real love, on the other side of the light which was attracting me so much. It was kind and loving and I remember thinking that's God.

Then I saw a hand reach through the light. I tried to touch it, to grab onto it, to clasp it so it could sweep me up and pull me through it." But just then his heart began beating again, and at that instant the hand's voice said, "It's not time. Go back and finish. It's not time." As the hand receded Sellers felt himself floating back down to his body, waking up bitterly disappointed.

William Peterson

William Peterson is the star of the T.V. show CSI, Crime Scene Investigation.

"Years ago, doing a play in Chicago, I cut my finger in half onstage. We obviously had to stop because, well, I didn't have a finger. By the time they got me to the ER I had lost a lot of blood and passed out. I could hear the doctors working on me, saying that they had lost my vital signs.

I was on the "All That Jazz" escalator with a long tunnel and a lot of white light. Then I specifically remember a dominant male voice saying, "It's not your time. Get off the escalator. You've got shit to do." I came to, and got sewed up. Something in me changed a sort of knowledge that somewhere on the other side, its good. For weeks, the more I talked about it, the more freaked out people got. Some of them were like, "Okay, whatever: You took too many drugs."

Tony Bennett

Tony Bennett is the iconic crooner who has reached an unbelievable level of success and a fan base that crosses generational gaps.

"A golden light enveloped me in a warm glow," he wrote in his autobiography. "I had the sense that I was about to embark on a very compelling journey. But suddenly I was jolted out of the vision ... I knew I had to make major changes in my life."

I actually had the pleasure of meeting Tony Bennett in the 1990's when I first moved to Las Vegas. I took a job as a security guard at the former Sahara Hotel and Casino. It was a Sunday morning and I was working the casino floor by the blackjack tables. Directly off this area was a small lounge and on Sundays they always had a live jazz band playing. The Pit Boss asked to tell the band to turn it down a bit since it was disturbing the players. When the band took a break, the members of the band were in a group off the stage talking. I walked up to the group tapped a gentleman on the shoulder and politely asked them to turn the music down per the request of the Pit Boss. The gentleman turned to me and it was Tony Bennett. He said "Tell the Pit Boss, no, I like it like this". I said my pleasure Mr. Bennett it is an honor to meet you and walked away. I delivered his response to the Pit Boss and needless to say the volume stayed just as it was.

Donald Sutherland

Mr. Sutherland played in numerous movies such as the Dirty Dozen, Kelly's Hero's, Kute, National Lampoons Animal House, The Hunger Games, The Italian Job and JFK as well as others. Perhaps one of his more notable roles was in the movie version of M.A.S.H. as Dr. Hawkeye Pierce. His NDE came when he had a case of meningitis in 1979.

"Suddenly the pain, fever and acute distress seemed to evaporate. I was floating above my body, surrounded by soft blue light. I began to glide down a long tunnel, away from the bed ... but suddenly I found myself back in my body. The doctors told me later that I had actually died for a time."

Ozzy Osbourne

While this may not be a shock, Ozzy "died twice" after a bike accident which left him in a coma for eight days.

"If it wasn't for Sam (my bodyguard) I probably wouldn't be here. He had to bring me back to life twice." Ozzy said. He described his confusion he had felt on gradually coming round from his coma. "I didn't know where I was or how long I'd been there. I would drift in and out of consciousness. Other times there would be a white light shining through the darkness, but no f---king angels, no one blowing trumpets and no man in a white beard."

Chevy Chase

Chevy Chase is from Saturday Night Live fame, also the movies Fletch, National Lampoon Vacation series of movies, Three Amigos, and the move Caddyshack.

Chevy was on the movie set for the movie Modern Problems when a scene went awry. He was doing a stunt and was nearly killed by being electrocuted during the sequence in which he is wearing landing lights and dreams that he is an airplane. The lights short circuited casing his NDE.

Other notable Hollywood Star who are said to have dad Near Death Experiences are:

Sally Kirkland – Actress of the movies Bruce Almighty, JFK, and The Sting and received an Oscar nomination for her role in the movie Anna.

Gary Busey – Oscar nominated for the movie The Buddy Holly Story.

Burt Reynolds – of Smokey and the Bandit fame and other iconic movie roles.

Eric Estrada – Best known for his role as a California Highway Patrol motorcycle officer 'Ponch' Poncherello in the T.V. show Chips.

James Cromwell - He played the role of Farmer Hoggett in the movie Babe. Some of his other credits are the Prison Warden in the Green Mile, Star Trek: First Contact, and LA Confidential.

George Lucas – the creator of the Star Wars movies.

Eric Roberts – The brother of Actress Julia Roberts.

Rebecca DeMornay – She played off of Tom Cruise in the move Risky Business she also played the wife in the made for television movie, the Shining in 1997.

14

Grief

I have given some thought to the Psychology of Death and Life and it ends with grief. I delved deep into my thoughts and my experiences that I have went through. I spoke of my thoughts with my therapist and as always I honor her opinion. I do listen to what she says even if I may disagree at times. But the discussion I had on my thoughts of death and life is based on the steps of grief and the journey to find myself and my 'being' once again. I felt that I have lost myself, although in my soul I knew I was the same person but with limitations. The best description of this path to find myself is that I was 'evolving'.

As humans, we are constantly changing. We always seem to have to adjust in one way or another. So the final determination is a path of evolution from what I was, to what I am or what I am going to be. So let's look at the steps of grief and how it affects the individual who is grieving the loss of a loved one as well as the loss of their former self.

This isn't just for the fortunate ones that have experienced heaven and returned. Grief isn't only for the surviving as they grieve the loss of a beloved family member. Grief is an emotion that those that face Post Traumatic Stress Disorder go through. There are the ones that unfortunately lost their ability to see or speak. There are those whose physical features were altered due to the tragedies of war or an accident or those that lost limbs to the violence of battle. But more so, there are the ones that have the mental anguish of what they saw and experienced.

Their physical being may be OK but the Post Traumatic Stress of their experience bears scars that cannot be seen. PTSD is not only for war veterans it is for all of us that have experienced a traumatic situation and we all must grieve for ourselves and our losses. I pray we all find peace within ourselves.

What is Grief?

Grief is a normal, sometimes painful, response to loss. The death of a loved one or the loss of a pet is the most common way we think of grief. Sometimes significant changes in a person's life can cause grief. Everyone experiences loss and grief at some time in their life. It is a reaction that we will all face at one point or another in our lives. The more significant the loss, the more intense the grief is likely to be.

We all experience and express grief differently. Some may withdraw into themselves and feel helpless, depressed and alone. Others may face grief with anger and want to take some form of action. No matter how one reacts, the grieving person needs the support of family and friends.

Grief has no time limit; the time it takes to overcome grief differs as much as the person himself. The process of grief is something that also needs to be understood by the person, family and friends. This will help with the psychological response to the loss and the grief one may feel.

The grieving person will experience different levels of grief which are described below.

Shock is typically the first reaction to loss. Shock is the emotional protection from being suddenly overwhelmed by the loss. The grieving person may feel stunned, or in disbelief concerning the loss. While in shock the person may not be able to make even simple decisions.

Suffering is the part of grief during which the person tries to gradually come to terms with the reality of their loss. The suffering process usually involves a variety of emotions, thoughts, and behaviors, as well as life seeming somewhat chaotic.

Sadness is perhaps the most common feeling found when one is grieving. It is often involves one crying. Sadness can become very intense and can be explained as having feelings of despair.

Anger can be one of the most confusing emotions for a person that is grieving. Anger can alter a person's basic beliefs about their self and about life in general. Anger is a typical response to feeling powerless, and frustrated. Anger may be directed at God, at the person feeling the grief, family and friends or at life in general. Anger can also avoid a person from grieving. Perhaps their pain is very deep so they become angry and the anger becomes their focus. If they focus on the anger then they do not have the time to grieve.

Guilt is a common feeling a person may have for hurtful things that were said, things that were left unsaid, or actions that were not taken that possibly may have prevented the loss or other damage that was done.

Anxiety can be a terrible part of grief. Anxiety can be nothing more than a small level of insecurity to causing severe panic attacks.. Often, the person that is grieving can become anxious about how they will take care of themselves following a loss. Anxiety is often accompanied by fatigue, loss of motivation, changes in how one is eating or changes in their sleeping habits, confusion, and loss of concentration.

Recovery and Acceptance, is the end result of grieving; it doesn't take away the pain or the memories of the one that was lost.

Instead, it is the reorganization of one's life so that the loss can be placed in another level rather than at the forefront of one's life. As recovery happens, the individual is able to resume a "normal" life.

They begin to gain a stronger attention span, gain more energy and resume with the activities of his or her life. The loss will always remain, but the loss has become part of the person's memories of their feelings and experiences.

Society has many misconceptions about grief, and may do so by making statements such as, "You must be strong", "You have to get on with your life", "Be happy you are alive", or "It's good that he didn't have to suffer." Saying things like this rarely help the person that is grieving. Grief is an individual emotion and as such carries its own time line. The best that family and friends can do is to be supportive and listen. The more the person in grief talks about it the sooner it may pass. This may not be easy but being a friend or a member of a family is often not an easy job.

Most people look at grief in the aspect that someone must have passed on to be grieving. When a person is diagnosed with a life threatening disease and becomes critically ill from this disease, they also must go through some or all steps of grief. When it happens suddenly the confusion of the process is moving rapidly and the person affected does not have the ability to grieve. They end up in a fight or flight mode.

When I look at the steps of grief, I realize I am going through the steps of grief myself. Unfortunately I am now grieving for the loss of my Mother and I am still grieving for the loss of me. I can see the confused look on your face right now. Let me explain what I mean by the loss of me.

When we go through a traumatic experience such as a death experience, we lose who we are. We were on a certain path; regardless of the path we have an identity, and a purpose. All of a sudden that stops. Our identity and our purpose change dramatically. What we knew about ourselves has stopped and our focus shifts to survival. There is nothing more, there is nothing less, just survival.

When you cross over and come back there is immediate shock, disbelief and confusion. You automatically flow into suffering and you feel the emotional pains of the confusion and the disbelief as well as the pain your body is feeling from the trauma it has suffered. The medications you receive for pain helps take away the obvious. What are left are the questions such as what just happened to me? Why did that happen? Will it happen again? The questions begin to pile up as you seek a solution to the questions and to the medical answers that are also compiling themselves. You find yourself in a Post-Traumatic Stress Disorder situation.

Sadness soon follows since there is a cross between happiness and depression. This does sound strange but it is a real feeling. On one hand you are happy that you have survived and you have another chance at life. You have another day with your loved ones and you can right some wrongs. Then there is the depression for what had just occurred to you and where you were and the amazing feelings you had there. The depression is also from the dramatic change in your life. Your identity as the person you were is now changed. You suddenly can't do what you used to do and that is often misunderstood by those that are close to you. These are traumatic mental adjustments to overcome.

This is the time when friends and family may say "what is wrong with you, why are you depressed? You are alive, you are here." What they do not understand is the complexity of the situation, the magnitude of what just occurred and the massive confusion in your mind.

There is nothing wrong with the living, they are just trying to help you but they can't understand because they have no capacity to process this information from the one that was dead, they never experienced it.

Anger, Guilt and Anxiety are the next three in the steps of grief. I have combined these three steps because I feel they coincide with each other.

You ultimately end up angry about what has happened to you. There may not necessarily be a good reason you are angry. There is the confusion and the feeling of your loss of control over your life. This can very well anger an individual because their identity has changed.

The Guilt comes in because your mind plays the game of guilt against its memory banks. If I didn't do this this may not have happened etc. You end up questioning all the things you have done.

All the while from the onset of shock, the anxiety levels build and get stronger. As you move through the mine fields of insurance companies, your job, the health care system, doctor appointments, additional medical testing and waiting on the results and then there is the financial part of it. The income changes and the stress of less income cause anxiety as well as guilt and anger to grow.

You may be able to get through it on your own, it may take some medication or you may need to speak with a specialist. There is no shame in speaking with a professional. The advantage of a therapist is they are a third party and do not have an emotional tie to you. They truly can help, but you must find the correct one. Once piece of advice regarding this, if you do not feel comfortable with the person you initially chose do not feel it is necessary to stay. Search out the correct therapist and your journey through this mine field of emotion and confusion and anger and sadness and depression will go more smoothly.

Recovery and acceptance then finds its way into your heart and your soul. You learn to accept what has happened, what you have been through and what the final determination is. It finds a nice safe spot in your memory and sits idle for times of reflection and challenges. You chose not to speak of it any longer since it has consumed your body and mind for so long. You seem to realize that anything that you may go through whether it is at your job, in your personal life are small in the grand scheme of things.

You have fought death and won this round. You have been through a massive state of confusion and you found your way out of the maze. You have a better understanding of the health care system and insurance companies and you are stronger and more educated because of it.

You realize that there are skeptics and those that simply are ignorant to the facts and refuse to understand. You know how to deal with these types of people and you are better for it. You have been there, you have crossed the line and you are still here to talk about it.

Your friends and family have not left you and you are finding your way back into the world. Society doesn't know of your journeys and you begin to blend into your old life but as a new soul.

Be Happy - You are a survivor!

15

Death Causes People to do Crazy Things

This chapter was an afterthought. While I was writing this book I was thrust into a situation that I knew would happen but I did not know when it would happen. After I experienced it, I felt it was necessary to tell the entire story since it did coincide with the subject matter of this book which is life, death, education and the dangers of free will here on earth. At the time I did not know I would enter this into 'Two Trips To Heaven' but because of what I was experiencing I started a this diary and that is what started this chapter. I will give you an advanced warning that what you will read is a story of unimaginable actions, destructive deeds, and some of the worst behavior I have ever seen in a family scenario such as this. I will also clarify that this is a true and factual series of events. It has not been embellished and it is so unbelievable that you just can't make this insanity up!

My Daily Log:

There is a saying that GOD doesn't give you more than you can handle. I am beginning to think there is no basis to this saying or GOD has a sick sense of humor. As I write this I am in Chicago at my Aunt Theresa's house because my Mother is deteriorating quickly and I had to place her in hospice care. As I stated in a previous chapter, the mind is a complicated computer and it somehow finds a way to cope, but sometimes it doesn't. My plate has gotten fuller and is now overflowing.

This is the time when faith is all you have to count on. I know this is a part of life but dealing with the present is difficult. I know this is best for my Mother. She is 93, she can't speak, she can't swallow properly, and her eyes are glazing over with a blank stare. No emotion is coming to her face any longer and what I have seen in the past few days in comparison to just a few months ago is as different as night and day. She is no longer active and her existence is simply that...... an existence. There is no such thing as a quality of life for her any longer.

It is her time to feel the joy and peacefulness of Heavens warm embrace and to see those who have long since passed on. I hope GOD will take her quickly into his arms and bring her home without any pain or suffering.

She has lived a long life and what we see now is a shell of her former self which is nothing like the woman she was with her vibrant personality and fiery ways and in no certain words would tell you exactly how she felt. She had no quims about saying to you in Italian "Ba fungul". (I will let you all Google that one) She was also very warm and loving and compassionate and giving. Everyone loved "Aunt Mary" and her passing will affect many in my family and in her community. She was that special woman that showed love for all who touched her life.

Saturday, January 12th, Day 1. My daughter and I arrived in Chicago and immediately drove to the Queen of Heaven Cemetery to insure my Mother's crypt was taken care of. We then went to Aunt Theresa and Tim's house. I picked up my Aunt Theresa and we went to see my Mother. She was sitting in her wheelchair, with no expression on her face. She had a blank stare and my daughter did not get any reaction from her grandmother. While Aunt Theresa stayed with my Mother, Tasha and I had to meet with the Hospice intake nurse to sign the paperwork required to start the hospice program.

Sunday, January 13th, Day 2. Today was much like the day prior. She was sitting in her wheelchair; she couldn't swallow the food she was given even in its puree form.

Her stare remained the same, no emotion to her face when I spoke to her. I could see the decline from a few months ago and it was difficult to grasp the dramatic change in her.

Monday, January 14th, Day 3. Today I had to meet with the hospice nurse that was assigned to care for my Mother and also the social worker from Hospice. This was a difficult day. We had to make the decision to remove her from her medications and I.V.'s and to allow the process of death to begin. This is when I learned the value of Hospice and saw their concern for my Mothers comfort in the last days of her life to insure she was not in any pain. Their empathy was also for us and how we will handle her imminent death.

I sat with both the nurse and the social worker separately and learned what will occur to my Mother on her decline of life and path to death. I feel it is necessary to list what I have learned so that others may understand the stages of death, what we will see and expect as the surviving family members when our loved ones are in Hospice care.

They were extremely thorough and did not hold anything back and that was appreciated. I found my spirituality very comforting at this time and as I learned more of the process of death in this fashion I was drawn deeper to my faith in GOD. I have never experienced this type of death. My first death was quick and just a matter of minutes from the time of the cardiac arrest started to the time I passed over to the other side. The second time it took hours for death to come and take me but in the grand scheme of death it was also quick. It wasn't days like I would see and witness what my Mother had to endure.

Death typically will come in stages once the Hospice program begins. The first stage is the person will begin to withdraw from their surroundings. They may become difficult to work with or simply become distant. My Mother was already in this stage when we arrived.

I was told that their minds will travel back to old memories and they may review in their minds the things they didn't accomplish or regrets they may have.

They may often apologize to those that they feel they may have wronged or forgive those that they feel have wronged them.

As they fall further into the steps of death their appetites will fall off and they will begin to lose weight. Because of their inactivity, their bodies will not require the nutrition it once did. Their liquid intake will also slow and their kidneys will slowly shut down as their urine output slows to a halt. At that point death is very close.

In the second stage their body will begin to shut down. They may feel colder than normal and they will sleep most of the time. It is similar to hyperthermia. The brain will realize the body is in trouble and the heart will realize the bodies' extremities are not as valuable as other critical organs and the heart and brain will work side by side to provide blood flow to critical organs. The mind is a complicated computer.

During this stage they will often be lethargic or possibly disoriented and even delusional. I saw this in my Mother; she seemed to stare at a certain spot and her eyes wouldn't move from there. It was as if she was staring at someone or something but we couldn't see it with our eyes.

Was she seeing my father, was she seeing her other siblings that have pasted on, was she seeing her parents? I will never know for sure, but I believe that is what was happening to her. Perhaps they were calling her home and telling her it is OK to leave us on earth and that we will get through this.

The final stage is when they are close to the end. I was told that she may appear to be responding again or have a short but sudden burst of energy. They may even get an appetite back when they haven't eaten for days. I didn't see any of that in my Mother. But I did see the next parts.

They will fall more into a trance like state and their breathing patterns will vary. The breathing will become shorter, slower and more irregular. They will also experience chest congestion where you hear a rattling like sound in their breathing that is called the "death rattle". The skin will begin to change color with the nail beds and lips turning a more blotchy purplish color first. That is another sign that death is coming quickly.

They also told me that their sense of hearing is the last thing to go. I kept talking to her and insured her that all of us here will be OK and that it is OK to go on and be with GOD. Speaking to them will help them in their transition. They will know they are not alone and they will know they are with those that love them and it will help them find peace before they know it is their time as GOD calls them home.

Then their breathing will become shallower and slower as the heart and lungs begin to shut down. They will draw shallower breathes until they draw their final breath of life and they reach a stage called Clinical Death. Although they have 'died' there is still the stage of biological death. Within 4-6 minutes of clinical death, resuscitation may be possible but some brain damage is likely.

Within 6-10 minutes of clinical death, if resuscitation is even possible, the brain will be damaged. After 10 minutes of clinical death, resuscitation becomes impossible in most instances.

That was quite a learning experience for me and compared to my death experiences, I realize how lucky I am that GOD didn't want me yet. Unfortunately we can't choose how we will die. But after learning this, I will prefer a quick death, so GOD when you do decide to take me for the final time, please give me the fast track home to Heaven.

Tuesday, January 15th, Day 4. My Mother is now on bed rest. Her body is very thin and frail.

Her age is clearly showing on her face and body and she is gasping for air although she is on oxygen. I was there with my daughter today sitting vigil. I hit a point where I could not take any more seeing her in this way. We spoke with her for 40 minutes more, and we got no response.

When we told her we had to leave for now she raised her frail skeleton like left hand. We held her hand, told her we loved her and everything will be OK here. She took a deep gasp of air and slowly exhaled. I thought that was the end but she started to breathe again. I lost it right there and broke down in tears.

My daughter isn't handling this well. I asked the social worker to come by tomorrow to talk to her. She is my concern and I want her to be able to get through this. She is the only grandchild and she was close to my Mother. I know and understand what will happen with my Mother.

I have accepted it although it is still a very difficult thing to endure. My focus right now has to be on Tasha to ensure she has a smooth transition to my Mothers subsequent death.

Wednesday January 16th, Day 5. Her decline is continuing. We spoke with the social worker today. I don't know why GOD won't take her but I am told by social services she will go on her own terms. That sounds more like my Mother anyway. She was quite the independent woman.

Thursday, January 17th, Day 6. Her condition is worsening. I returned by myself this evening and sat with her and talked to her. I told her about the events of April 2012 and what had happened to me. Not that I wanted her to worry in any way but I wanted her to know the greatness of Heaven. She is preparing to take this journey and I want her to find peace with letting go. I held her hand and told her about Heaven and she squeezed my hand hard.

She wouldn't let go, and I felt this was her way of accepting what I was telling her. I felt she understood the glory that was awaiting her and it was her way of saying goodbye to me, until we meet again.

I took a special picture of our hands. It is quite a powerful photo and that moment is one that I will cherish more than any other time we had spent together.

Friday, January 18th, Day 7. I had a strange interaction with Aunt Theresa this morning. This is getting weird. Tasha and I went to see my Mother this morning, but, my Mother was still very lethargic. I can see the steps that were described to me by the Hospice people taking affect. I felt Tasha needed a break from this sad vigil so I took her to the Shedd Aquarium for a few hours. Once we returned to the nursing facility later in the afternoon, my Mothers breathing had become more labored. The hospice nurse said death was coming and it could be hours but no more than a day at the very best.

I went and picked up my Aunt Theresa so she could see her sister, my cousin Tim and his Daughter Jackie were there and a close friend of my Mothers, Samantha, was there as well as my daughter and me. They stayed until about 9:30 PM. I remained for about an hour more but finally succumbed to the helplessness. It is so difficult to see your loved one as life is being removed from their body by each breath and death is circling just waiting its turn. Once again you are helpless and have no control of this situation. I returned to the house and in typical Italian fashion, we made pasta, drank some wine and talked until about midnight or so and then I retired from an exhausting day.

The call came from the nursing facility at 1:45 AM that her breathing had become shallow. I woke Tim and Tasha, Tim didn't want to come and Tasha and I arrived at the nursing home at 2:03 AM.

Today is Saturday, January 19th, day 8 in Chicago. As I write this it is a cool 37 degrees in Chicago with temperatures due to drop into the 12 degree range Monday and Tuesday. It is now 3:15 AM. I just returned to the house from the nursing facility. My Mother lost her battle at 2:10 AM this morning.

We arrived to see her as she was taking her last few shallow breaths. I called my Aunt Theresa about 2:30 AM to let her know that it was over, my Mother had passed away.

Mary's journey to the other side had begun and I can only hope and pray that her transition was as blessed as mine and even more so because she was truly a deserving woman to be in the arms and glory and grace of GOD.

It has been a difficult week and this is when family is most important, the death of a beloved family member. We all had our own levels of stress. We all handle death differently, but we must all remember there are others that are just as affected as you are and possibly more so. But death makes people do crazy things.

As in situations such as this, some of the family gathered by my Aunt Theresa's house in the late afternoon of the 19th. My cousins Charlie and Sandy and John and Joyce came by and in typical Italian fashion food was in abundance. The sadness of her passing was also filled with the joy that she was out of the agony she was in. We celebrated her life as most Italians do; with food and drink and many stories. It still hasn't really sunk in yet that she has passed on. In time I am sure those feelings will come to the forefront.

Today is Sunday the 20th of January, day 9. Theresa had serious attitude this morning and I reached my breaking point. I told my daughter I was leaving for the day. I didn't have any more room on my plate or my shoulders. My wife will fly in this afternoon. I can use her support right now. I have a few last minute details to handle with the funeral home, check us into a hotel for a couple of days and tomorrow, Monday, the 21st of January is the wake and the Italian heritage of death begins.

⚜

Unfortunately, with death there is a business side. Not only is this book written as a spiritual experience but I do offer advice on certain topics from firsthand knowledge. Of course all decisions are yours and yours alone.

Lesson #1. Do not use emotion to choose the services and casket etc. People tend to buy with emotion at this extremely emotional time. I would suggest, if possible, that you bring someone with you whose mind isn't full of sadness, shock, grief and possibly remorse and they know how to say the word 'NO'.

Lesson #2. One thing I have learned while working in the 'burial business', is that the funeral isn't for the one that passed on, it is for the ones that are living.

Lesson #3. Stay within a budget. Remember that the $1,200 casket will serve the same purpose as the $5,000 casket and will look just as wonderful during the wake. Once they are buried it will never be seen again.

Lesson #4. If you are doing an in-ground burial, take one step up for the vault. Do not buy the least expensive vault, spend the additional couple of hundred dollars for the water proof version, it is worth the value.

Lesson #5. Do the one day wake or the same day service. Keep the obituary notice to a minimum. The funeral home knows how to nickel and dime you. Remember, the funeral business is a for profit business!

The Church was my biggest shock. The church is a non-profit organization and as such gets special tax exemptions. Tax benefits for religious organizations fall into a few general categories: tax-free donations and tax-free land. (There may be as much as $100 billion dollars in untaxed church property in the United States) For every dollar which the local governments cannot collect on church property, it must make up for by collecting it from citizens.

Thus all citizens not only pay higher property taxes but are also forced to indirectly support churches, even though they do not belong to them and may even oppose the church or religion in general. The words, separation of Church and State do not seem to apply here.

My Mother was a devote Catholic and a volunteer in her church for over 30 years. She freely gave her time to help others and help the church. I wanted to give her a proper Catholic funeral so I contacted her church. The days of a 'stipend' are apparently gone. The Catholic Church now has a menu price list for a funeral. The use of the church is $275.00, the altar boys are $20.00 each, the organist is $100.00 and the cantor (singer) is another $100.00. I was told "these are very good prices and some of the lowest in the area!" (Ah, the sales close, I almost felt like I was on the used car lot) The days of the church being a caring and giving place whose concern is ministering to its flock is a thing of the past.

Now I do not want to offend the devoted Catholic followers whom may be reading this. That is not my intent. Do not forget I was born and raised a Catholic and an Italian Catholic at that. I was quite upset by the numbers I was given for a one hour funeral mass for a 30 plus year member of the St. Domitilla's parish. My Aunt Theresa was upset with me that I was angry at the church and my cousin stated the church is struggling and they even had to shut down their Catholic School. My heart was touched also. I expected to give a 'stipend', what I did not expect was a menu price list. Is this the reason the following of the Catholic Church is declining? Are people seeing this isn't about the love of GOD but more about the love of money?

Lesson #6 is negotiating. Ask for discounts etc. The funeral director has room to move but he won't if you don't ask, just like the car dealer.

Ask a lot of questions and see what his answers are then make a reasonable decision based on facts, your available funds and not emotion.

I was even able to get a little money off the price of the funeral and also a little bit off the price of the church. Now, I do not want you to think I am cheap. But when the church gave me a price list it went from respect for the church and became a business transaction and in business, we negotiate!

My one regret is not being an organist. Think about the numbers; she apparently doesn't have a full time job since she is older and plays the organ for the church at funerals and weddings and masses. The mass will last 1 hour and she earns $100.00 and may play 5 songs, $20.00 a song isn't too shabby. She will miss a few episodes of Judge Judy, but for $100.00 an hour I would also. Did you know the average pay for a member of the Chicago Symphony Orchestra is $144,000 per year? Now between performances and practice, if they put in a 40 hour work week they earn $69.00 per hour. So, $100.00 an hour isn't a bargain for a non-professional musician.

This story about the Catholic Church is my sole impression and opinion based on what I experienced. However, I do believe that the church is a business and it is not determined by the denomination of the church. Of course the decisions are yours and yours alone, so choose wisely, go with your heart and do what you feel you need to do and what you desire to do.

I am an only child and unfortunately I had to handle the arrangements by myself. The stress level was elevating and I had no outlet or release. It is OK, I am a man, and it is my sole responsibility. I thought I would have some moral support but that never came to fruition. I must understand that some people can't handle stressors the way I can, but, I'm not handling this one well at all.

Monday, January 21st, Day 10. This is the day of my Mother's wake. We arrived early to view her body before others came. She looked so much better! The funeral director, Mike Bruno, did a fantastic job. He has been our family funeral director for as long as I can remember. He must be nearing 90 years old and is still as sharp and active as ever. The man is an artist that truly loves his work. He does it all, from start to finish. As far back as I can remember he has been handling the deaths in our family. The first I can remember was my Grandpa Pete in 1968. I know there were some before that also.

❦

My Mother's funeral didn't turn out to be about my Mother as it should have been. I realize my Aunt Theresa also lost her sister but the funeral turned out to be about my Aunt Theresa and her loss and had nothing to do with 'our' loss or my Mother.

I realize that was a difficult statement. Situations like this happen more often than not but typically it is more behind the scenes than in the forefront. Allow me to explain.

Many little things happened along the way and many little things will eventually grow into one big thing as it did in this case. This is a book for the populous so we can learn of my death experiences, the transition to Heaven and the wonderment and freedom that death does bring. It also discusses the struggles of the free will on earth that causes so many issues. As unfortunate as this was, it also holds lessons in the experience of death, so this story will be told. All of this actually happened! Once again, this is so far from normalcy that you can't make this stuff up!

All of these little items added up and caused a small rift between us but there is another more serious matter that involved two large diamond rings my Mother used to wear that tore us apart. To understand this on a deeper level, let's look at a few statements that were made.

Five years ago when my Mother went into the nursing home, Theresa stated that she wanted my Mother to "wear them (the two diamond rings) in the casket." I agreed with this and at that time and saw no harm in Theresa holding the rings in Chicago. After all she is my Mothers sister and my Aunt, why wouldn't I trust my Aunt? If this was in fact her intent and something my Mother may have wanted, then why did she not comply? Things that make you wonder?

We had a conversation at the kitchen table the morning before my Mother passed away and I asked her if we can get the rings to place on my Mother while she was in the casket.

She replied in a loud and angry voice: "Those rings belong to your daughter and grandchildren". This was not the question I asked but, OK. My daughter was sitting right there, she was in the State of Illinois, in my Aunts house for 10 days. If honoring my "Mothers request" was such an important factor in my Aunts heart then why not get the rings and give them to my daughter within the ten days she was there? It isn't as if my daughter lived in a surrounding suburb in Illinois where she could swing by casually one day in the next week or two. My Daughter lives in Tennessee and won't be back to Chicago anytime soon. Theresa didn't honor my "Mothers request". Things that make you wonder? My Mother already expressed to me what her wishes were 5 years ago and I must say that there is a difference of opinion.

On Saturday, January 19th, after I made the final arrangements for the funeral and returned to the house, Aunt Theresa asked me if I bought flowers for my Mother.

I stated that I bought a casket spray for my Mothers coffin that said Mother, Grandmother and Great Grandmother and then she asked me why I did not get a rosary shaped casket flower spray. When I asked why that mattered, she stated because "I wanted to keep it". I was a bit perplexed by that response.

One of the first things Theresa said to the funeral director when she arrived at the funeral home on Monday while pre-viewing my Mother as my wife, my daughter and me were standing there, was; "I WANT that rosary" (the rosary in my Mothers hands).

I know it may sound petty but this is my Mother's funeral, I brought that rosary specifically for my Mother to be buried with from a few rosaries that I had of hers back in Michigan. All she had to say was; "Rob, I would like the rosary to remember your Mother" and it would have been done, no questions asked. My Daughter saw the Theresa way of logic and then started the same thing, "I want........." It was like vultures picking the bones clean. Why must people act this way? I was taken aback by what I was hearing. This is the start of my Mothers wake!

My Aunt and my Mother belonged to a senior club through the village and church for many years. The seniors would get together, play cards and take little excursions etc. Many of the seniors came to pay their respects and not once did Theresa introduce me to any of them as Mary's son as I stood by the coffin. Would it not be appropriate and respectful to introduce me to the members of the seniors club? After all I am the deceased's only child. Once again, it was all about her loss not ours.

My Aunt never asked me one time how I felt about losing my Mother. Not one time was that question raised to me, although I did ask my Aunt on numerous occasions if she was OK? That was out of respect. Once again it was all about her loss not ours.

I also don't have a problem with which songs should be played or sung or who does bible readings etc. The whole family could have done the entire mass. Seriously, it doesn't matter to me! But, I already spoke with the church and relayed my wishes when I wrote the check for the funeral mass. Apparently while in the coffee room of the funeral home she was making the decisions on who would do what readings etc. As I stated it doesn't matter to me but it wasn't mentioned or discussed with me. What if I already chose other people? It was done without any respect for me. Once again it was all about her and her lose.

Since I am the one paying the bill wouldn't it be proper to mention things to me? All I wanted was a touch of respect in this difficult time and I received nothing. There were no such courtesies relayed to me and it was as if my wife, my daughter and I were not part of this funeral or feeling any of this loss.

Now before you ask, "wait, why do you keep saying you are paying the bill? Wasn't there life insurance and isn't that what the life insurance is for?" Yes, there was a small policy that barely covered the funeral expenses. But I am still the beneficiary of that policy, am I not? How that money gets spent is my decision as the beneficiary, correct?

I was trying to honor what my Mother wanted. I could have done what others have done (I will not mention names) and not had a wake, had her cremated immediately and placed her urn into the mausoleum space with my Father and been done with it. But, that wouldn't be the right thing to do so I did the best I could to honor my Mothers burial wishes on limited funds. So with that being said, let's move on.

I was astonished at the lack of courtesy regardless of the fact that this was her sister. I could not understand why there was the need to act this way and have the need to be so disrespectful. This was adding so much stress to my already highly stressed body. I didn't have much room left to take on much more. It doesn't simply stop there.

There is much more and it gets crazier as the story goes on. As I stated before this is so out of the norm that you simply can't make this stuff up!

It was also recently brought to my attention by a member of my family that I didn't provide a meal after the funeral for those that attended. The correct wording was, "you had an opinion on the meal after the funeral, but we made it work". I want to clarify and specifically state that it was not stated to me in a mean spirited way. I am not offended, but it was stated none the less.

I don't know what they expected of me. The unfortunate part is no one comprehends that my Mother was indigent, I haven't worked in 10 months and I am on disability collecting only a small portion of what I used to earn and that does nothing but pay my immediate bills. My Mother also never owned a home as her other sibling(s) do or did and as such there is no property to be able to sell, and no inheritance to gain. I also do not have a sibling to assist with any of this and all that was left in her bank account was $336.31 which barely paid for the church service which ended up being $320.00, (since I negotiated it down).

Another point of interest that was brought up to me and again not in a mean spirited way was, and I wish to quote this for clarity; "Mom and Tim had you to the house and did all they could. I think they felt a bit slighted for their efforts." I would love to know what that means. Since Tim and his Mother aren't on speaking terms with me I suppose I will never know.

Now, in my defense, when I got the call to come to Chicago, I immediately contacted Tim. I asked Tim if we could stay there during this process. He could have said no, he could have said it wouldn't be convenient, he did have that option, but my request was granted. Isn't that what family should do at a difficult time like this? I then contacted my daughter and ex-wife.

My daughter does not have any money so I had to pay for her to fly to Michigan so we can drive to Chicago together because long distance driving is still difficult for me because of the dizziness. Now in all fairness, I did not realize it would be 8 days but my wallet was always open and contributions were made and the receipts are available for review. My daughter helped Aunt Theresa and I maintained dignity and politeness.

Could you imagine if I called my Aunt Theresa and said "the nursing home called me and my Mother is dying, she can die within the next week or two and we need to put her in Hospice, they are faxing me the papers to sign to place her in Hospice care and I will come in when they call and tell me she has died. But, no big deal, I will handle the funeral arrangements when I get there." If I did that, combined bible verses come to mind.

The locust would have sprung from the earth with the powers of scorpions, the winds would have howled with rage and the rain would have fallen from the heavens for 40 days and 40 nights so the earth could be cleansed from evil and I would have been cursed and placed on the same platform with Satan for all of eternity.

Well, apparently doing the right things did a lot of good, Satan and I now share top billing in some people's eyes.

Once again it may be a petty thing, but for someone who proclaimed her grief at the loss of her sister in such a fashion as she did, one would think a simple bouquet of flowers would be appropriate for her beloved sister, none were sent. Once again it is something I remember and something that others have conveniently dismissed as irrelevant.

Here is one of life's lessons that I remember well and it is a very simple lesson; if you want certain things you can either politely ask the responsible party for them or you can pull out your own check book and pay for what you want! She did neither.

The dispute concerning the two diamond rings was also coming to the forefront. Please understand that this is about items that did not technically even belong to my Mother or any other member on that side of the family. The diamond rings came from my Fathers guardian, Reta Wagner who was basically his Mother and my grandmother. She and her husband Al Wagner raised my Father after his Mother passed away when he was about 8 years old. Reta had a stroke and was living with my Mother and Father in my room and I was living upstairs in my Grandma's apartment. Then a few months before my Father passed away she had another stroke and had to be placed into a nursing home. That is when my Mother came into possession of the two rings in question.

Two weeks after my Father passed away, Reta died also. We had back to back funerals. I was 19 years old at the time. When Reta died she left a sizable estate in excess of $1.5 million. For years and years she always told my Father and I that we are her heirs. No will was found and based on that, her estate went into probate. Probate discovered that all her stocks, property and life insurance policies had herself listed as the beneficiary. That caused some legal issues of custody that could have been explained and worked through if my Father was alive. Since he died 2 weeks earlier, it was then considered hearsay regardless of what was said to me and regardless of what I could prove about his life. As such, and without a will, I lost a sizeable estate and walked away with virtually nothing.

Theresa was a vile woman and refused to produce the diamonds for me as I am the legal heir of my Mothers estate. If I am not alive then that right goes to my only child, Tasha. Once again, it is my responsibility and my decision but yet again, I was being disrespected and set aside like a bad piece of baccala (salted cod fish).

Lesson #7. Make sure you put it all in writing and trust no one, even members of your own family. Never in a million years would I have expected my Mothers sister, my Aunt, my 'brothers' Mother and the wife of my Godfather to act in such a deplorable and disrespectful manor.

I know that all her siblings and parents in Heaven were turning in their graves at her actions up to that point, especially my Mother. She wanted nothing to do with me or my wife for the remainder the funeral. It was even overheard as we were walking the casket into church that she didn't want to sit close to us. She slid the knife into my back so quickly that it was unconscionable. But, the worst was yet to come.

Death Causes People to do Crazy Things.

As they say, actions speak louder than words. For some reason she felt it necessary to show me ZERO respect in my Mother's death. All of this showed me that my feelings and emotions were irrelevant to her. I was of no concern in her mind and I was her sisters' only son and her husband's Godchild but that didn't matter one bit. Her loss was the only thing that mattered. One must remember that not only in the Italian heritage but in all heritages that RESPECT is a key aspect in a family. If you give it, it should be returned. I gave it to my aunt and nothing was returned to me or members of my immediate family.

The stress level from that problem, words between my daughter and my wife, watching my Mother lose her battle to live seeing her draw her last breath all took a toll on me and my health. My plate was overflowing with stress.

Once we left the funeral home and prior to the procession to the church the finality of my Mother's death began to hit me hard. In the car I mentioned that Aunt Theresa didn't even acknowledge us at the funeral home. My wife made a comment and my daughter fired off some choice words to my wife.

Tasha stormed out of the car and went to the car my Aunt was in and ran her mouth to her, which caused further tension in this family. I certainly did not need this on top of everything else on this day of all days. All I wanted to do was to give my Mother a proper wake and funeral and burial.

As we entered the church my grief was growing. My wife and I placed the church funeral blanket over the casket and tears were streaming from my eyes.

We sat in the pew and I was overwhelmed with severe grief. The funeral mass had begun and the priest is performing the service. I began to hyperventilate and was on the verge of syncope. My wife and Tim's girlfriend, Becky, were able to assist me in gaining some control by slowing my breathing. That lasted a few minutes then another wave hit me again. This time it felt like a heart attack and my left arm and leg went numb. My cousin Tim saw the distress I was in and asked me if I was OK, I shook my head no and he called the police and paramedics.

The funeral mass is in full swing and I can't breathe, my wife is scared, my daughter is scared, the priest seemed to speed up the mass. The paramedics arrived and checked my pulse and it was over 125+ beats per minute. My blood pressure which normally runs 100-110 / 65-75 was elevated at 169/98. Then the left side of my face went numb and I knew I was having another Transient Ischemic Attack (mini-stroke). With my medical history they advised me to go to the hospital. I refused to leave my Mother's funeral.

My Aunt in the pew in front of us never turned around once to see if I was alive or confirm that I was dead. How cold hearted does a person have to be to do that? Not that it mattered but it just showed more bad behavior and proves my point that I mean nothing to her.

My daughter leaned over and was talking to me to try and calm me. I said to her, "Tasha, fix this". (The issue with my wife) Then she stormed off to the other side of the church kicking a kneeler on her way and was heard cursing. My cousin Charlie turned and gave her a look of death and that bad behavior halted immediately. More stress I did not need on the day of my Mother's funeral. Why does death cause people to be insane?

Lesson #8. Blood may make you related, but Loyalty makes you family.

More bad behavior occurred as we were waiting for the funeral procession to the cemetery. As I was sitting in the car shaking, my wife went up to Tim to talk to him about a text she sent him the night before. She was worried that all this stress would affect my health and it had. Tasha then rolled down the window of Tim's car and tried to speak with Lisa. Lisa stated that tensions were too high and she was going to speak to her today. Then my daughter called her an "evil bitch". I cannot for the life of me understand this incorrigible behavior. It was just more bad behavior that I did not need on the day of my Mother's funeral. Then another female cousin comes up to my car and starts to talk to me about these rings. First of all the timing wasn't appropriate and secondly she is not involved in this what so ever so why she felt it necessary to even involve herself in that discussion was very wrong and just caused me to have more stress. At the cemetery chapel I was shaking as I was standing at the casket. After the final prayers I was taken to the hospital for an evaluation. Tim and Lisa were with me.

When we arrived at the hospital, my heart rate and blood pressure were still elevated. They checked my blood enzymes and gave me a CAT scan of my head to see if I was in the midst of a stroke. Tim and Lisa were both visibly upset as they were working on me and they left the room, and went to the waiting room and apparently Tim told

Lisa some personal information and stories about his childhood, his Mother etc. It apparently was a nice moment that they were able to share. The two most important people in my life seemed to have found a level of trust.

I was then placed into a hospital room and the care stalled. The hospital confirmed a T.I.A. and after my 2nd cardiac enzyme test was negative they determined I had an anxiety attack not a heart attack.

I had a standing appointment with my neurologist in two days and after the third cardiac enzyme test was negative and the CAT scan results were negative I decided to check myself out of the hospital so I can return home to see my personal physicians.

When I returned to the hotel about 10 PM, I sent Tim a text that I was going to leave in the morning and I needed to stop by his Mother's house to pick up some flowers, some frozen beef and the rings. He responded, "I need a break from all of this, please let me be." I respected his request. As I said earlier, the worst has not happened and is yet to come.

Day 12, Wednesday, January 23, Lisa and I were leaving and heading home to Michigan. I left Lisa to pack up as I had to sign some papers at the funeral home about 10:00 AM. I then went to pick up the items from my Aunts house. I arrived about 10:30 AM. Let's just say her actions were unbelievable and shocking. The extreme bad behavior that I faced in the midst of my Mother's death was unheard of and I can honestly say we are still in complete shock by the actions of this member of my family.

As mentioned earlier, I texted my cousin the night before, and notified him that I needed to go to his Mother's house. He didn't want to be bothered and I honored his wishes. I knocked on her door and rang the bell. I did not pound on the door; I did not continuously ring the bell, nothing of the sort. I saw her peek out and said "I see you Aunt Theresa I want to get the flowers."

As I said before, this gets worse.

She did not respond and I went back to my car and immediately called Tim, his phone went directly to voicemail. I then sent Tim a text immediately stating, "Tim, at your mothers alone to pick up the flowers. She won't open the door saw her peak out the window. Come on man not looking for a fight just want to get my stuff and go."

As I backed out of the driveway a Hillside P.D. officer was in the middle of the street, he activated his overhead lights and I pulled up alongside the police car and was asked if I knocked on that woman's door. I said "yes, she is my Aunt, we buried my Mother yesterday and I need to pick up flowers and things. I just stayed at her house for 8 days, so she knows who I am." He asked if I would walk up there with him and of course I said yes. We pulled the cars out of the street and walked up to the door.

When she opened the door it was immediately known that I wasn't an "unknown man" to the police officer. She was very angry and vile and the first thing she stated was "I don't want him in my God damn house!"

A second officer arrived just moments later and came in the house as I was getting the frozen Italian beef I had in the basement refrigerator and I was collecting the flower arrangements from the funeral that I wanted to take home. I asked her for the rings and she once again angrily said "you will never get those rings they are for your daughter!" I did state calmly in return that I am the legal heir and I would get a lawyer involved if necessary.

The second officer asked me, "Aren't you the guy from St Dom's yesterday?" It was the officer that came to the church when Tim called for assistance.

I told him yes and he asked if I went to get checked out. I stated I did and was diagnosed with an anxiety attack and I had a Transient Ischemic Attack (TIA).

I asked the officer to help carry the larger bouquet of flowers for me which he did and I collected my things and left.

I did send a fee to secure a copy of the incident report from the Hillside Police Department. The incident report states everything above and also states that there is a dispute concerning the rings in question.

The important part of this report by the police officer is what his report stated: "I was assigned to the Xxxxxx residence, 123 Some Ln. on a report of an ABANDONED 911 call with no answer on the call back. While en route to the call I was advised by dispatcher Smith (not his real name) that he made contact with a female resident who called because there was an unknown subject knocking on her door."

Her reaction when she opened the door to the police officer showed the "strange man" story was nothing but a lie and that shows she did this out of anger and revenge nothing more, nothing less. If she was indeed fearful for her safety, she would have not hung up the original 911 call and she would have remained on the phone with 911.

In essence it did in fact show that she was not in harm's way at all or it would have been stated on the report and I would have been questioned and/or arrested, which I was not. As Judge Judy always says, "If it doesn't make sense then it is not true." Her story did not make sense.

I cannot even imagine my Mother, Aunt Sue, Aunt Arcy, Aunt Chicky, Aunt Millie, Aunt Ethel, or Grandma calling the police on any of the cousins ever. That is devastating and horrible. I could only think what my Mother was saying right then? I thought I heard a "Ba Fungul Theresa" but I wasn't positive. I also thought I heard Uncle Sam's powerful voice saying "WHAT IN THE HELL IS WRONG WITH YOU THERESA?", but, I may have been mistaken.

I can only say that her actions were unforgiveable, insulting, bordered on ignorance and done for no other reason except out of anger and revenge. She was an extremely angry and vile woman in her actions that day and I believe Satan would have got a warmer welcome than I did.

Stress put me over the edge and I did yell at my cousins, Tim and Sam on the day of the funeral I did apologize to Tim for my inappropriate behavior at my Mothers casket. I also apologized to Sam on two occasions.

I also apologized to other members of the family that may have taken some things I said incorrectly. If a member of my family is reading this book, and if you feel slighted, it wasn't out of disrespect so please accept this as my apology.

Death Causes People to do Crazy Things.

I am working through the events of this experience and I am still in shock and disbelief as to what has occurred and is unfortunately still continuing. I have a cousin who I consider a brother that won't speak to me. We have traveled together for over 15 years for our birthdays; we would talk 2, 3, and 4 times a week. We confided in each other and by all accounts were extremely bonded together. After I returned home and was going through a few of my Mother's boxes, I found an old yearbook from when I joined the Navy in 1977.

A letter fell out of it, from him, talking about coming down to Florida when I got out of boot-camp which shows how far back we go together.

As I finish this book, it has been more than 2 months since my Mother was buried. I have not heard a word from him except a message relayed by his brother for me to not contact him. I ask myself why and for what? Since there is no communication I can't speculate on the reasoning. It is just another thing I must accept.

Time will tell all, but actions affect time.

Death Causes People to do Crazy Things.

Remember these words and try to accept certain actions that are out of the norm by some people. It may take time to heal; it will take time to grieve as we all grieve in different ways. Time is the ultimate healer for most of us and for a select few time never heals the wounds and anger becomes their standard of the day.

I have gone back and forth for weeks on whether I should tell this story in full detail. I originally was not going to discuss the events of the funeral and of Wednesday January 23. I planned to leave the mystery on the table for you, the reader.

After the events leading up to this point and realizing the terrible behavior of this event I felt it necessary to tell the truth and explain the insanity of not only this day but this entire funeral experience. I know some may read of this and say that there is no way that any of that happened. They may say I must be embellishing these facts. I have no reason to do any such thing. I have no reason to lie and I am not writing this to hurt anybody. I am writing this because of the shear insanity of it all.

It is so unbelievable and so far out of belief that not telling this story is more detrimental to the readers. Let me give you just a tad of background on how our family intertwines and perhaps you can understand all of this just a tad better.

Christmas Eve was the main holiday that the family got together for at Grandma and Grandpas house. After they passed on my Aunt Arcy and Uncle Eugene took over the tradition and did a great job of keeping the vast majority of the family together for many years. Some years some were not in attendance, other years another group wouldn't be there but overall the family was together. When Arcy and Eugene passed on the family finally splintered.

Uncle Tony and his crew pretty much stayed on the South side, Sue and Angelo would have their own family and some of Arcy's kids, and Uncle Pat and his group would have their own Christmas and my Mother (and me when I was in town) would spend Christmas with Aunt Theresa and Uncle Sam and their family. That went on for many years.

My immediate family and Aunt Theresa's immediate family were very intertwined for many, many years. That is why I am still very astounded by the actions that took place during and after my Mother's funeral. I feel that if this high level of insanity can happen to us, then you should be warned. It can happen to your family also.

❧❧

I would imagine that a majority of readers are awed by this story at this point. I told you before this got worse and we haven't hit that spot yet.

It isn't like the lines of communication were wide open where we could communicate like adults and come to an acceptable conclusion. No one has communicated with me about this situation since February 6th when I expect that the details of the conspiracy was concluded. On the 18th of February I was told by my ex-wife that my Aunt is sending her the diamond rings. I know I asked my cousin to not involve Debbie or Tasha in this on at least three different occasions and I know I told Debbie and Tasha that they are out of this equation on two separate occasions.

But once again my words were not heeded and I was once again disrespected. I don't get the connection except that she is my daughter's mother. She is a third party, not related, and has not been a member of this family for 30 years. But it is more bad behavior by my Aunt Theresa. She would rather send them to a woman she hasn't seen in 30 years than the rightful heir. But I had no other option but to accept this since no one from that side ever communicated with me. Just more bad behavior!

I don't know why no one else is communicating with me on this situation, and although I did not want my ex-wife involved in this I had no other option since the transfer was in process. I asked my ex-wife to let me know when she receives them and to not break the seal of the package and to forward them on to me. That would also complete the rightful line of inheritance. By doing that it would also keep her out of the loop if something is amiss. She readily agreed and I thought we were settled.

Death Causes People to do Crazy Things.

She called me and told me she has them, she opened the package and now doesn't wish to forward them to me and wants to hold them for the grandchildren. Now the battle starts over again. Another person who is NOT part of this situation putting in their opinion on a matter that does not involve them. This is between me and if anyone, my daughter. I spoke to my daughter in detail about my wishes and how this should be handled a couple of days ago and we were in agreement and now a new twist suddenly is involved.

I called my daughter and tried to talk some sense to her and I also told her straight as I have always spoken to her, to make it right or lose my phone number. She will get them when the time is right. Then my daughter emails me and tells me she is keeping them and that is that (I wonder where that sudden influence came from?) This may sound petty to some but I would expect the vast majority of the readers to think that the events that are taking place is a horrible display of dysfunction and I, once again, agree with you on this.

I had no problem making a will and having it notarized that those rings will go to my granddaughters when I die. I already agreed to that but that apparently isn't good enough. The issue isn't about the rings or what will happen to them or the value of the rings as you have read. That bus has left the station. It has turned into the greed of people who do not have a horse in this race.

The issue now is based on deceit, lies and disrespect. Why would a child (well, she is a 31 year old adult) take a stance about items that are not rightfully theirs. She took our relationship and tossed it aside by deceiving me and lying to me because of impatience and I frankly don't know what else got into her head. As a father, that hurt deeply.

Per Illinois law; the Rules of Decent and Distribution under Illinois law state; "The intestate real and personal estate of a resident decedent and the intestate real estate in this State of a nonresident decedent, after just claims against his estate are fully paid, descends and shall be distributed as follows: (b) If there is no surviving spouse but a descendant of the decedent: the entire estate flows to the decedent's descendants per stirpes."

(In English) Since there are no other siblings and no surviving spouse, what she had flows to me as her sole heir and further distribution is at my discretion.)

Now what are my options? I sought out the logical advice of a couple of my older cousins that are not involved in the matter. I took the advice that was given to me which was to write down all the options and the positive and negative effects. Nothing will come out of any of the options that will be of any good. So the goal was to find an option that will have the least amount of fall-out.

It has gotten too far past that because some wouldn't communicate and involved others that should have not been involved. It is all due to lack of communication from the member's in Chicago, lack of honesty, lack of respect and lack of common courtesy. This is such a sad and disturbing turn of events. And you all thought it couldn't get worse?

I considered just letting it all go and let sleeping dogs lie. On the other side, that would only park the issues to be brought back up at another time, another place and not put this to rest ever.

People will be happy for only a short time. Holding all this in would also be detrimental on my physical and mental health. Then again maybe I could find peace within myself and let it go for the sake of my health. I would not be able to mend anything with those involved knowing the high level of deceit and conspiracy that took place. Of course no relationships can be saved.

I have considered civil action against all of those involved. You can't reward bad behavior. I am correct according to Illinois statute and I feel fairly confident that I would win in court and then I would place significant lien amounts on their houses. The other side is it will cost money and additional travel expenses and of course no relationships can be saved so I do not see an advantage to this option.

I also realize there is no hope of negotiating with any of them for a solution so; once again I am between a 98 ton boulder and a 98 ton rock. Well, there you have it, this is the most dysfunctional situation in the wake of a death that I ever have heard of.

There aren't any options that can solve this issue at this point in time. Damage has been done and it seems that it is now irreversible. All because of the anger of an old woman, lack of communication and no compassion.

Since I have returned home I have put my final wishes in writing. I have done a living will, a medical power of attorney; I have laid out my intent on being alive in a state of helplessness.

I have put forth my wishes for my burial, the funeral home I want to use and the cemetery and burial arrangements I prefer. I also have it down to what jewelry I wish to have on in the coffin and what I want to be buried with.

I am also currently working on my Last Will and Testament. I will leave nothing to chance but I am sure somewhere, somehow, some words and disagreements will raise its ugly head after my death but I will insure to the best of my ability in accordance with the law that nothing like this can possibly occur.

This is the downfall of free will and greed when it comes to death and why?

Because...............

Death Makes People do Crazy Things

Death Makes People do Crazy Things

Death Makes People do Crazy Things

Death Makes People do Crazy Things

Death Makes People do Crazy Things

Death Makes People do Crazy Things

Death Makes People do Crazy Things

Death Makes People do Crazy Things

Death Makes People do Crazy Things

Death Makes People do Crazy Things

Death Makes People do Crazy Things

To My Mother

Dear Mom,

I did the best I could. I know I wasn't always around and that I lived out of state for the majority of my life. I couldn't be around at times when you may have needed me. But I always called you; I always tried to help when I could. I visited as often as possible and I was there for any major medical issues you were facing. When the facility told me I better come, I did without question.

I was with you when you began your decline and I was with you when you took your last breath of life. I tried my best to give you the wake and funeral you so deserved. I hope you were proud of what I was able to do for you regardless of all of the insanity that transpired and is continuing.

You will always be remembered, revered, loved and you will be sorely missed. I will carry these events with me to my grave and grieve over them every day but most of all I will grieve for you; as you gave me life, you always stood at my side and always loved me regardless of my misgivings.

Mary Noble..............Rest in Peace.

This book is dedicated to your memory.

16

Just Another Story

In my particular situation, the doctor appointments and medical treatments and tests have gone on and on. I am now in month ten of these trials and tribulations. Since April 2012 I have had five Esophagogastroduodenoscopy (EGD) procedures, a T.E.E. procedure to check the back of my heart and a surgery to implant a loop recorder above my heart. The ulcer in my stomach is growing and getting larger and deeper and it is infected. Since we can't determine the cause of the ulcers and my system is not responding to the medications, I met with the surgeon on Feb. 6th to discuss a surgery called a vagotomy along with a poliotomy to cut the Vagus Nerve in my stomach which is over reacting and producing too much stomach acid which is causing the ulcers not to heal. As always we will run a few more tests before we make the surgical decision. I am comfortable with that decision but the options are running out and doing nothing will eventually lead to another internal bleed out when the ulcer perforates the stomach wall.

The CAT scan showed I have a nodule on my thyroid and a calcified nodule in my left lung. It never ends. I had an ultrasound to follow up on the nodule and the radiologist say there is no nodule. Well, that may be so but how talented is the guy who is reading the scan? So, we have one radiologist reading a cat scan saying there are nodules and another reading an ultrasound saying there isn't.

Talk about confusion. So, the bottom line is, someone is wrong. We have conferred with the surgeon and I do not have a thyroid problem. Thankfully this is one less challenge of my plate.

When I left the hospital in May of 2012, I had a difficult time walking up stairs, I couldn't shower without assistance, and I would be in Home Depot with my wife and would have to sit on the floor because a syncope episode was knocking on my door. We would be at a little local restaurant and I would get numb and dizzy just sitting at the table. The summer heat would limit my ability to be outside because my body would overheat. When we were on the boat and I overheated, I would have to get in front of a fan in the cabin or put cold towels on my head and neck to bring my body temperature down.

Since then I am doing better. My strength is up, the episodes are much less frequent, I can handle the heat better, I can perform basic household functions and I can drive again. I still do not drive long distances alone but I have improved. I still get a bit dizzy now and then and I still have challenges catching my breath. When I wake in the morning I still need to sit on the side of the bed for a minute or two or I will end up on the floor but I have improved or at least I am learning how to deal with this.

Time is healing the physical wounds to my body and for that I am thankful. The emotional and mental wounds are much deeper and taking much longer to repair.

I do not know how much longer this will go on. There are still things pending. The fact is it doesn't matter how much longer this will last. I cannot change it, I cannot control it, and I can only accept it. After extensive and continuing therapy I have learned about control. I am learning to handle the things I can't control and how to work with things that I can control.

"God grant me the serenity to accept the things I cannot change;
Courage to change the things I can;
and wisdom to know the difference."

This has become a daily mantra.

I have spoken to my therapist in depth about the issues I faced in Chicago at my Mother's funeral and what happened at the Church during the service. I do agree with her assessment which is; my body told me that enough is enough and there was no more room for any more distress. I have never been like that at any time in my life. I have never had an anxiety or panic attack, I have always been able to handle adversity of any levels and move forward.

But, this time is different. I feel lost, confused, disappointed, and I do not have the energy to fight any more and medications are the only thing that keeps the devil away from my soul at this time. Her advice is to let everything go and only handle the things that are extremely necessary. It is now confirmed that I must postpone the surgery for three to six months until I can be released by Neurology and hopefully be capable to emotionally, physically and mentally handle the stress of a major operation and the surgeon agrees. Since that is the case I will return to work and try to move forward with my life and I hope and pray my body will be able to handle the pressures of the work environment.

When you are used to having a level of control in your life and suddenly life as you knew it has virtually shifted overnight, you are left in darkness. It is a darkness that you rarely witness throughout your life. It is helplessness, sadness and loneliness. You must find your way through the forest in all its depth and despair. The paths you take sometimes split and your path gets clogged and the vines get thick but you must fight your way through the thickness to get yourself back on track. It isn't an easy path but with determination, courage, spirituality, and rest, it allows your body to heal. You will find the end of your path and you will eventually come out of the forest. It may take weeks or months or longer. Your time will come.

As time goes on, the pain, the discouragement, and the confusion subsides and your life begins to return to normal; whatever the definition of normal may be. Soon, what you have been through and what you have felt in your 'Near Death Experience' and beyond will only be a memory.

It will be an event you will never forget but it is also something that will not come up in conversation any longer and it slowly allows you to be who you are and your life will move forward.

In most instances the Near Death Experience doesn't require additional medical actions or treatments. Your Doctor appointments become less frequent and all you have are general follow-up appointments. In my case, my doctors do not know what else they can do at this point in time and I must try to find my normalcy if I can.

You may think of it now and again. There will be the moments when you are alone and the quiet takes you down that that dusty old road in your memory. But you are able to park it and keep moving forward with your life here on earth. Your memories of your trip to the other-side are still holding a prominent place in your memory and you may find yourself smiling at the thought of how great that transition felt and you know in your heart and your soul that you will one day feel the love of GOD, the wonderment of Heaven and the peace of the transition once again and you will be thankful to be back in the arms, grace, and glory of GOD.

Your work life continues on, holidays come and go and before you realize it the weeks, months and years pass you by. Your children and grandchildren grow older as do you and what was at one time the main focus in your life is nothing more than a distant memory.

What has happened to you, just becomes...........another story.

No Mas

17

Bizarre Death and
Burial Facts & Epitaphs

*The Atlantis Memorial Reef or Neptune Memorial Reef is the world's largest man-made reef located off the coast of Key Biscayne, Florida. Ashes are mixed with concrete to create a reef underwater, known as the Neptune Memorial Reef or Atlantis Memorial Reef (an underwater mausoleum for cremated ashes).

*When Thomas Edison died in 1941; Henry Ford captured his last dying breath in a bottle.

*When Mahatma Gandhi died, an autopsy revealed that his small intestine contained five gold Krugerrands.

*Robert Hershey, of Hershey Chocolate fame, died when he fell into a vat of chocolate and drowned.

*In 1845, President Andrew Jackson's pet parrot was removed from his funeral for swearing.

*When Mark Twain was born on Nov 30, 1835, Halley's comet was visible over Florida and Missouri. Mark Twain predicted in 1909 that he would die when it returned. He was right. When he died on April 21, 1910, Halley's comet was once again visible in the sky.

*Adolph Hitler's mother seriously considered having an abortion but was talked out of it by her doctor. (more bad medical advice)

*American Jim Fixx, the man who started the trend of jogging, died of a heart attack while out jogging.

*King Charles VIII of France died as a result of his gallantry. On entering a tennis court in 1498, he bowed to his wife and allowed her to proceed first. As he brought his head up, it crashed against a low wooden beam, fracturing his skull and killing him.

*Escape artist Harry Houdini boasted that his stomach could withstand any blow. But one day a fan punched him without warning. Houdini collapsed in agony, having suffered an internal rupture. He died shortly afterwards.

*More people are killed each year by coconuts than sharks. Approximately 150 people are killed each year by coconuts.

*Nutmeg is extremely poisonous if injected intravenously - it can kill you.

*There are 5 times as many deaths due to the negligence of doctors as there are deaths due to firearms.

*Only one in two billion people will live to be 116 or older.

*When a person dies, hearing is generally the last sense to go. The first sense lost is usually sight followed by taste, smell, and touch.

*On average, right-handed people live 9 years longer than left-handed people.

*More people are killed by donkeys annually than are killed in plane crashes.

*A properly folded military flag shows 4 stars, one each to represent the Army, Navy, Air Force, and Marines.

*Taberger's safety coffin was designed in 1829. It included a bell to ring that would alert the graveyard workers if they were being buried alive.

*Elephants and chimpanzees both have been known to bury their dead, by throwing leaves and branches over the deceased members of their families.

*Queen Victoria insisted that she should be buried with the bath robe worn by her dead husband, Prince Albert. Even stranger, her royal highness took an actual plaster cast of her beloved Albert's hand with her to the grave.

*The late, Hollywood icon, Judy Garland, shocked the world when she died of a drug overdose in 1969 in London. She was displayed for public viewing in her glass coffin and more than 20,000 fans came to pay their respects.

*"I am ready to meet my Maker. Whether my Maker is prepared for the great ordeal of meeting me is another matter."
The last words of Winston Churchill

*Princess Diana's sudden death in 1997 saw her funeral ceremony pass an estimated 1 million mourners through the streets of Westminster, London. 2.5 Billion People watched it on TV across the globe and saw Elton John sing a rewritten and personalized rendition of 'Candle in the Wind'.

*Due to the inherent lack of space and money in China, most people opt for cremation over burial.

*In 1992 Playboy founder Hugh Hefner purchased the crypt next to Marilyn Monroe for $75,000. He said, "Spending eternity next to Marilyn is too sweet to pass up."

*Each year the United States buries enough caskets to equal 30 million feet of hardwoods, 90,272 tons of steel, 2,700 tons of copper or bronze

∽◦∾

Strange Epitaphs

"Here lies Lester Moore, Four slugs from a forty-four. No Les, No Moore."
Boothill Cemetery, Tombstone Ariz.

∽◦∾

"Here lies John Yeast, Pardon me for not rising."
Cemetery in Ruidoso, N.M.

∽◦∾

"I Told You I Was Sick"
Cemetery in Key West, Fla.

"In loving memory of Ellen Shannon, aged 25,
Who was accidentally burned March 21, 1870,
By the explosion of a lamp filled with R.E. Danforth's
Non-explosive burning fluid."

Epitaph in cemetery at Girard, Pa.

⌒ᴅ⌒

"The children of Israel wanted bread
And the Lord sent them manna,
Old clerk Wallace wanted a wife,
And the Devil sent him Anna."

In a Ribbesford, England, cemetery

⌒ᴅ⌒

"Here lays Butch,
We planted him raw.
He was quick on the trigger,
But slow on the draw."

In a Silver City, Nevada, cemetery

⌒ᴅ⌒

"I was somebody.
Who, is no business Of yours."

Someone determined to be anonymous in Stowe, Vermont

"Here lies
Ezekial Aikle
Age 102
The Good
Die Young"

❦

"Here lies an Atheist
All dressed up And no place to go."

In a Thurmont, Maryland, cemetery

❦

"Sir John Strange.
Here lies an honest man.
And that is Strange."

A lawyer's tombstone in England

❦

Famous Epitaphs

Merv Griffin - Broadcaster - TV show Host – Producer
"I will not be right back after this message"

Rodney Dangerfield – Comedian
"There goes the neighborhood"

Jackie Gleason – actor – comedian
"And away we go"

Mel Blanc – the voice of Porky the Pig and Bugs Bunny and 100's of others.

"That's all folks"

Billy Wilder - screenwriter, director and producer of over 60 films.

"I'm a writer but then nobody's perfect"

Jack Lemmon – actor

"Jack Lemmon in."

Frank Sinatra – singer – entertainer – actor

"The best is yet to come"

Dean Martin – singer – entertainer – actor

"Everybody loves somebody sometime"

Sammy Davis Jr. – singer – entertainer – actor – dancer

"The Entertainer He did it all"

Jesse James – 1800's outlaw

"Murdered by a traitor and a coward whose name is not worthy to appear here."

Al Capone – 1920's gangster

"My Jesus Mercy"

Robert Frost - four-time Pulitzer Prize winner for poetry

"I had a lover's quarrel with the world,"

Bette Davis – actress – entertainer

"She did it the hard way"

Allan Pinkerton – law officer – found of Pinkerton security
"A friend to honesty and a foe to crime"

Minnie Riperton Rudolph – singer
"Loving You is Easy Cause You're Beautiful"

Sonny Bono – singer – entertainer – politician
"And the beat goes on"

The grave of the Unknown Soldier in Arlington National Cemetery
"Here Rests in Honored Glory An American Soldier Known But to God"

Ed Wynn – actor – voice actor – Best known for the voice of the Mad Hatter from Alice in Wonderland. Later, he played crazy Uncle Albert in Mary Poppins.
"Dear GOD: Thanks"

Martin Luther King Jr. – clergyman – activist - leader in the African-American Civil Rights Movement.
"Free at last. Free at last. Thank God Almighty I'm Free At Last."

Wyatt Earp – 1800's law man – business man
"Nothing's So Sacred As Honor And Nothing's So Loyal As Love"

John Quincy Adams – statesman – U.S. President
"This is the last of Earth! I am content!"

Studs Terkel – author – Pulitzer Prize winner – historian – actor – radio broadcaster
"Curiosity did not kill this cat.

Jim Morrison – singer – entertainer

"Truth to your own spirit"

W.C. Fields - Entertainer

"Here lies W.C. Fields. I would rather be living in Philadelphia."

Alexander the Great

"A tomb now suffices for him whom the world was not enough"

Wyatt and Josephene Earp

"nothing's so sacred as honor and nothing's so loyal as love"

Robert Frost

"I had a lover's quarrel with the world"

Blood makes you related – Loyalty makes you family.

Blood makes you related – Loyalty makes you family

Blood makes you related – Loyalty makes you family

Blood makes you related – Loyalty makes you family

Blood makes you related – Loyalty makes you family

Blood makes you related – Loyalty makes you family

Blood makes you related – Loyalty makes you family

'God grant me the serenity to accept the things I cannot change; courage to change the things I can; and wisdom to know the difference.'

About the Author

Robert Noble still resides in Michigan and is still married to his wonderful wife Lisa. They still find ways to enjoy their lifestyle with their two faithful dogs, Zoey, a Beagle and Roxanne, A Brat Terrier (half Boston / half Rat Terrier) and their Iberia Greek Tortoise, Sheldon.

As of this writing he not yet returned to his employer but has plans to return within a two month period. He is trying to adjust and maintain while still working through some of the medical challenges.

The pain and disappointment of January 2013 is still prevalent and the pain and disappointment of February is now taking center stage. He is still in complete disbelief but he will not take much more. He now hopes as each day passes a bit of the pain falls away also. He still is trying to decipher the depths of the fall out but that too, with time, will work its way out.

Robert still believes that there is a much better place besides this existence here on earth. He believes that here on Earth is where we atone for our sins and we must fight free will that will be used to damage our faith and find free will that will advance our spirituality. We are not perfect beings and will have to answer for our actions. So think about that and pray for forgiveness for the bad you have done and caused.

Your life is a spiritual journey and 'free will' will and can alter your path. It is what you do with your decisions that will decide your fate at the hand of GOD.

GOD Bless You All

www.ingramcontent.com/pod-product-compliance
Lightning Source LLC
LaVergne TN
LVHW021458080426
835509LV00018B/2332